87 SECRETS OF
OUTRAGEOUS
BUSINESS SUCCESS

"You are someone I've grown to admire greatly. You share your knowledge with and encourage people in achieving their dreams, trying new things, and learning tricks of the trade. It's a rare 'guru' in our world today who is thoughtful and kind enough to help up and comers find the path to success. In my opinion, you are the very best. I'm grateful to you."

—Linda Capriotti

"During the past 20 years, Bob Bly has become one of America's leading direct response copywriters. He has probably done more to teach other writers the craft of effective and persuasive writing than anyone else."

—Roger C. Parker

"After considering a number of high-level marketing professionals and reflecting on the matter for several weeks, I made the decision to ask Bob Bly to share the stage with me for my Twin Keys to Wealth-Building Conference. The reason I chose Bob is because I am convinced that he can deliver more tangible value to conference attendees than any other marketing or Internet expert on the planet."

—Robert Ringer, best-selling author

"I love your e-mails. Read every single one of them as they come in."

—Dr. Paul Hartunian

"I receive so many e-mail offers — too many — but Bob always delivers a product worth having. The marketplace for writing and marketing products has become over-hyped; in that environment it's reaffirming to see that Bob continues to stand for a level of quality that matters — and happily, at a price that works. "

—Peg Prideaux

"Watch Bob Bly very closely. He's a very intelligent marketer who knows how to get results and bring in the money!"

—John Kidd

"I have enjoyed all of the books that I have read of yours. I appreciate your no nonsense, take-it-to-the-bank advice that you deliver."

—Nicholas J. Loise, RSVP Chicago

"The Handbook and your bonus are first class. I'm very pleased. You never disappoint."

—Louis J. Wasser, Copywriter

"The product promos you've been sending have plenty of content. I look forward to your e-mails, because they are great idea generators. And your price points are very reasonable. I'd rather pay from $29-$97 for one of your products than the $299 - $500 I've been dishing out to others. Your current business model is brilliant and fair."

—Stanley M. Jackson

"I am delighted every time I take one of your recommendations! You haven't steered me wrong once, and each of your products has been well worth every penny invested."

—Pat Johnson

"I learn a lot from your e-mails even when they point to other products or products you sell. I like learning. Keep it coming."

—Pat McKenzie

"Yours are one of the e-mails that I do enjoy and I order from you as often as I think I can use the help."

—Joe Alagna

"I eagerly anticipate your e-mails — all of them. I've made several purchases. You offer a lot of great advice and insight free. You offer a lot of [other] great advice and insight at very reasonable prices, typically with immediate delivery. Personally, I wouldn't want to miss the opportunity to consider anything you think might be helpful."

—**Linda Byam**

"You develop a helpful product, describe it in detail, make it easy to access online, post a reasonable price and offer a money back guarantee. Personally, I thank you for your contribution. I've purchased many of your products. And I've made returns. You stand by what you sell, plus."

—**Lynn Roberts**

"What we receive free from you and others has the potential to ignite countless ideas - priceless ones on occasion. The opportunity to in turn purchase something from the 'sales' e-mails is complimentary to you sharing so much priceless info with us — your willing subscribers. Press on and keep allowing us to benefit from your years of experience however you share it."

—**Eddie Stephen**

87 SECRETS OF OUTRAGEOUS BUSINESS SUCCESS

HOW TO REACH YOUR GOALS
AND HAVE FUN DOING IT

ROBERT W. BLY

NEW YORK

87 SECRETS OF **OUTRAGEOUS** BUSINESS SUCCESS
HOW TO REACH YOUR GOALS AND HAVE FUN DOING IT

Published in New York, New York, by Morgan James Publishing. Morgan James and The Entrepreneurial Publisher are trademarks of Morgan James, LLC. www.MorganJamesPublishing.com

The Morgan James Speakers Group can bring authors to your live event. For more information or to book an event visit The Morgan James Speakers Group at www.TheMorganJamesSpeakersGroup.com.

BitLit
FOR ALL THE BOOKS YOU OWN

FREE eBook edition for your
existing eReader with purchase

_____

PRINT NAME ABOVE

For more information, instructions, restrictions, and to register your copy, go to **www.bitlit.ca/readers/register** or use your QR Reader to scan the barcode:

ISBN 978-1-61448-681-7 paperback
ISBN 978-1-61448-682-4 eBook
ISBN 978-1-61448-683-1 audio
ISBN 978-1-61448-902-3 hardcover
Library of Congress Control Number:
2013947015

Cover Design by:
Chris Treccani
www.3dogdesign.net

Interior Design by:
Bonnie Bushman
bonnie@caboodlegraphics.com

In an effort to support local communities, raise awareness and funds, Morgan James Publishing donates a percentage of all book sales for the life of each book to Habitat for Humanity Peninsula and Greater Williamsburg.

Get involved today, visit
www.MorganJamesBuilds.com

Habitat for Humanity®
Peninsula and
Greater Williamsburg
Building Partner

For my sons,
Alex and Stephen

TABLE OF CONTENTS

ACKNOWLEDGMENTS

Thanks to those subscribers to The Direct Response Letter who asked me questions and suggested topics that sparked the essays in these chapters.

INTRODUCTION

For years, I've published a twice-weekly e-newsletter that goes to about 65,000 subscribers.

Originally I dispensed strictly marketing advice. But then I broadened the scope to encompass more areas of business success and life in general.

As soon as I did, the reaction from subscribers was immediately and overwhelmingly positive. So I've continued to write my twice-weekly e-mail essays.

Eventually, I self-published a few of the essays as an e-book. Terry Whalin, an acquisition editor at Morgan James, read the e-book. He then suggested we add many more essays and bring it out as the paperback book you now hold in your hands.

Is this the best advice in the world on business, entrepreneurship, marketing, copywriting, freelancing, and Internet marketing? Probably not, but it is the best I can give you, based on my experience as a marketer, entrepreneur, and writer since 1979. You can read my bio at the back of the book, along with testimonials from my e-newsletter subscribers, to determine whether I am worth listening to.

I continue to write and distribute the essays online, so if you have a question, e-mail it to me and I may, if I feel qualified and able, answer it in a future issue: rwbly@bly.com

In addition, you can get all my future e-mail essays free by signing up for my e-newsletter here: www.bly.com/reports. When you sign up, you also get 4 free bonus reports totaling 200 pages with a retail value of over $100. Details are on the sign-up page.

It's my hope that by reading this book, you will in plain and easy-to-read language get advice and ideas that can help you:

- Get better ROI from your marketing campaigns.
- Generate more clicks, leads, and sales on the web.
- Start and run a successful Internet marketing business.
- Start and manage a successful career as a self-employed professional.
- Write more clearly, engagingly, and persuasively.
- Manage your time better and improve your personal productivity.
- Achieve a more harmonious work/life balance.

I sincerely believe that even if you only get one good idea for improving just one of the areas named above, it will pay back the modest cost of this book tenfold or more — not a bad return on your reading investment.

1

VALUE YOUR TIME

The other day subscriber WK sent me an e-mail asking if we could have lunch:

> "I'd like a chance to meet you, if possible, just to meet so that sometime in the future we might be able to work on something together," wrote WK. "I live in northern NJ so we aren't so far apart. I've probably been in your neighborhood many times."

I get asked to lunch by subscribers who live in or near my area a few times a month. And I always say no.

Here's why I won't go to lunch with WK or even you, as much as I may like you:

1. I find going out to lunch in the middle of a work day to be an enormous drain on my severely limited supply of time. I would rather spend the time working.

2. Many subscribers try to tempt me by saying the lunch will be on them.

   I charge hundreds of dollars an hour for my time. Do you think paying $10 for my tuna sandwich and Diet Coke is really a tempting bribe for me?

   Some people up the ante by offering to take me to an expensive restaurant. This plea falls on deaf ears; I don't care that much what I eat and fancy restaurants don't appeal to me. And if I desire an expensive meal I can well afford to pay for it myself.

3. I am introverted and even reclusive by nature. I have no desire to eat lunch with someone I don't know.

4. WK says we should meet "so that sometime in the future we might be able to work on something together."

   If WK or anyone else wants to work with me, we do not need to meet to make that happen.

   I virtually never go to meetings; all my work is done via FedEx, fax, mail, and e-mail.

   I rarely leave my desk during the day. And I almost never travel, except for seminars.

5. Should WK want to ask me for advice, he can do so by e-mail or phone, and I will gladly answer short questions at no charge.

   A question I could answer in 2 minutes on the phone or by e-mail would take up an hour or two of my time at lunch.

The fact is there are very few things in my life I value as much as my time.

Not money. Money can be replaced. If you lose money, you can always make more of it.

But time is irreplaceable. Once it's gone, it's gone for good. You can never get it back.

If I spend 2 hours having lunch with WK, that's 2 hours away from doing my client work ... or writing my book ... or spending time with my family ... or doing other things I like to do.

This is why I have never been big on joining committees for clubs, business associations, and the like — they suck up precious time that could be used for more rewarding or pleasurable activities.

One of the best ways to not squander your precious, limited time is to learn to say "no."

"No, I can't have lunch with you."

"No, I can't attend that meeting."

"No, I can't serve on that committee."

"No, I can't volunteer to serve in that capacity."

My attitude may raise your hackles or offend your sensibilities.

That is not my intention.

I am not telling you what to do or how to live your life.

But people ask me how I am able to get so much done in my life — a continual stream of copywriting projects, these 2X weekly e-mail articles, columns, seminars, information products, 80 published books and counting.

It is by valuing, conserving, and protecting my time like it was gold in Fort Knox — and learning the magic of saying "no."

2

GET PAID FOR
YOUR INFORMATION.

The late Aaron Swartz, who co-created the RSS Web feed system when he was only 14, believed that in the Internet age there should be no need for anyone to pay for the information they want.

"Information is power," said Swartz. "But like all power, there are those who want to keep it for themselves."

I don't want to keep my information for myself. But given the time and cost required to create my publications, aren't I entitled — just like any other working stiff — to be compensated for my labors?

"The world's entire scientific and cultural heritage, published over centuries in books and journals, is increasingly being digitized and locked up by a handful of private corporations," Swartz wrote.

By "a handful of private corporations" I think he means publishers and other content producers. Publishing is a for-profit business, like any other.

"Sharing isn't immoral," Swartz continued. "It's a moral imperative."

In every case? I don't believe the U.S., for example, willingly shares its military secrets with its adversaries.

Nor do competitors within an industry share all their trade secrets with one another. Are they morally corrupt not to do so?

Swartz concluded: "Only those blinded by greed would refuse to let a friend make a copy."

I don't consider myself greedy, but I do not allow my customers to copy my e-books and give away those copies to their friends.

That would be a copyright violation; they would be stealing from me.

If their friends want my e-book, they can pay the same $29 per copy everyone else does.

The Internet has encouraged what author Harlan Ellison told me is a "slacker mentality."

It has also caused more people to take the position that all information should be free — which conversely and necessarily means authors and other content creators shouldn't be paid.

I find this position patently absurd.

No one expects her dentist to fill her cavities for free ... or her dry cleaner to press her skirts and pants without charge.

So why should writers, designers, programmers, composers, and other content creators be required to work for free — and give up any chance of making a living from their craft?

It is unfair. It makes no sense, Swartz to the contrary. In America, in a free market, workers get paid for their labor.

Already, the Internet has created a marketplace where content writers in particular are expected to work for peanuts.

A recent article in The New York Review of Books stated that the average Mexican journalist gets paid a paltry $5 per article!

When I started freelancing in the early 1980s, the going rate for article writing was $1 a word.

How can you survive as an author or content creator in the "information should be free" Internet mindset?

Here are my suggestions:

1. Do not become a commodity writer. If a thousand other writers could write the piece you are working on approximately as well as you can, you are a commodity writer.

2. Those most in danger of being commodity writers are content authors who are generalists — that is, they write about a broad range of topics, moving from subject to subject based on their mood and the jobs available.

3. You can increase your worth in the market by specializing in a niche. That specialization can be by medium (e.g., Web sites), audience (e.g., writing for baby boomers), or subject (e.g., writing about oil and gas exploration).

4. The narrower and more specialized your niche, the easier time you will have getting work and the more you will be paid.

5. Focus on writing projects whose purpose is to generate leads or sales for your client; e.g., e-mail marketing, direct mail, landing pages, banner ads. Reason: clients whose projects generate leads or sales view writing as a profit center, not a cost center.

6. You can maximize your compensation when you handle assignments where the increased revenues your sales copy generates can be precisely measured. That way, the value of your copy is beyond dispute.

7. Create an overwhelming demand for your writing services through proactive marketing that generates inquiries and self-promotion that establishes you as an expert in your niche.

IS THE CUSTOMER
ALWAYS RIGHT?

One of the worst things you can do when paying good money to hire a copywriter is to change his copy and then run it without letting him know.

Why is this bad?

Because even a small change in the wording can significantly depress response.

I have seen the change of a single word in a headline or subject line lift or lower response in an A/B test by as much as 10% to 25% — and occasionally by 50%.

On more than one occasion, clients have told me that the copy I wrote for them didn't work.

Then, when they send me the promotion, I see that the headline or some other key piece of the copy is not as I wrote it — almost always an unpleasant surprise for me.

The client rewrote it without telling me — and then amazingly tells me that "my" copy didn't work. Ha!

Preventing this is easy as pie.

Just send your copywriter a PDF proof of the promotion before it runs.

That way, he can:

1. Check it to make sure nothing important has been altered.
2. Get a fresh reading and possibly suggest last-minute changes that make it even stronger.

Does this mean you will never have a losing promotion again?

Not at all.

Any honest marketer or copywriter would tell you that a significant percentage of promotions simply do not work.

But making sure any important changes are carefully reviewed and well thought through does increase the odds of having a winner in your favor.

H.G. Wells once said: "There is no greater human urge than the desire to rewrite someone else's copy."

Having a client change or rewrite my copy is not a problem for me when I believe the altered version is as good as — or better — than what I had written.

When it's not, I tell the client why I object to the revisions.

But if he still wants to make the changes after hearing my reasoning, I acquiesce pleasantly.

After all, it's his money.

Questioning the work of the professional you hired is not unique to copywriting, by the way.

Doctors, for instance, increasingly say that their patients are doing more of their own research online — and challenging the doctor's opinions and recommendations.

It seems a bit odd to me that in an era of specialization we doubt our specialists more than ever.

The Internet may be the reason: people think they can get the same expertise their experts have just by Googling the topic, which is absurd:

They get the information but not the knowledge, skill, and experience in how to apply it.

Certainly, the explosion of copywriting training available — books, courses, coaching programs — has made the average consumer of copywriting services more knowledgeable.

Syms, a local retailer, says "an educated consumer is our best customer." I know I enjoy working with clients who understand what I am doing.

Taking the opposing point of view, JL, my gray-haired tile guy, told my wife when she suggested a change in his tiling technique: "A little knowledge is a dangerous thing."

4

EVALUATING CUSTOMER
COMPLAINTS.

My subscriber SM was confused or possibly upset by my endorsement of the AWAI copywriting course:

http://www.thewriterslife.com/bobrecommends

The source of her consternation was her finding a discussion board where a contributor bashed the AWAI course and me for recommending it.

"You happen to be one of the top names out there, and your opinion counts," SM wrote me. "This got me pretty confused."

My message to SM is: there's nothing to be confused about.

You know the old saying: "You can't please all of the people, all of the time."

SM seems to have forgotten it.

My friend, motivational speaker Rob Gilbert, has a formula that encapsulates this maxim:

SWL + SWNL = SW

This stands for:

"Some will like you, your services, or your products. Some will not like you, your services, or your products. So what?"

You cannot control people's preferences, tastes, and beliefs.

All you can do as a marketer or service provider is to work diligently to find out what people want from you ... and then tailor your products or services to deliver it.

Even then, you will not please all of the people, all of the time.

Yet SM seems to think you can and must.

"I saw many positive reviews upon research, and this one negative review (admittedly only one), just knocked it all out," she writes.

That makes no sense to me, because it's to be expected that some will like you, your services, or your products — and some will not like you, your services, or your products.

Why would SM think otherwise?

My advice for interpreting criticism, ratings, or reviews: throw away the worst review and the best review, and take the average of the rest as your true ranking.

I do this when evaluating my performance in giving seminars.

On the evaluation, I ask the attendees to rate me on a scale of 1 to 5, with 1 = low and 5 = high.

Mentally, I disregard the highest score and the lowest score.

I throw out the best evaluation because there are some people out there who seem to be rabid fans of your stuff beyond what is rational: they just love whatever you do.

I throw out the worst review because there are some people who hold an almost irrational grudge against you: they hate your voice, your face, your ethnicity, your philosophy.

At one seminar an attendee gave me a bad rating because he thought my shoes were not highly polished enough. I am not making this up.

(Years later I was at a Toastmasters event where one of the club members, giving a talk on how to succeed in business, said that one of the most important factors was to wear expensive shoes that are well polished.)

You may want to go through a similar process when evaluating any set of critiques, reviews, or comments; i.e., Amazon stars for a book, a debate on a bulletin board, e-mail from product purchasers.

It will give you a more accurate and reasonable assessment of the quality of the item under discussion.

One critic on the anti-AWAI discussion board gave this advice: "Any time you are thinking of taking a course, type the course name into Google followed by the word 'scam' and see what comes up."

This is terrible advice.

Reason: any time a really successful person offers to sell advice on how to duplicate his success, it raises the ire of envious and skeptical people who believe such a thing just can't be so.

The reason for their skepticism is often that the results the marketing promises — and the author and his students have actually achieved — are just so far beyond the readers' experience that they simply cannot believe it is true.

Subscribers often ask me, "Can't people just put fake testimonials on their Web sites?"

Of course they can, but most don't, because it's not only unethical but also illegal, and the penalties are stiff if you get caught.

5

HOW TO DRESS FOR SUCCESS: THE LOST SKELETON OF CADAVRA

The classic sci-fi spoof movie, "The Lost Skeleton of Cadavra," was on TV last Sunday.

In the movie, an alien tries to fit in with human society by trading in his space suit for a jacket and tie.

"This neck-restraining device is uncomfortable," he says, tugging at the tie. "I wonder what its purpose is?"

I mention this because it was my having to wear a tie to work every day that was one of the primary reasons I decided to quit my job and become a freelance writer in February 1982.

I think most people who take the leap from corporate employment to self employment do so for the advantages: they want to make more money, have more fun, or do more creative work.

But I became a freelance writer because of all the things it would help me avoid:

- No more commuting.
- No more having to wear a suit and tie.
- No more having to shave every day.
- No more meetings or business travel.
- No more having a boss.
- No more office politics.
- No more depending on a single company for my annual earnings.

Of all these, believe it or not, the one I disliked most was wearing the 1980s working uniform of a suit and tie.

Technical writing guru Peter Kent once commented that the only function he could see that wearing a tie served "was to restrict the blood flow to the brain."

I am a big believer that, both in your dress and your surroundings, you should take pains to make yourself as comfortable at work as you can possibly be.

The simple logic is that if you are comfortable, you will enjoy yourself more, and if you enjoy yourself more at the office, you will stay there longer.

Here are some things that can make you happier and more comfortable at work; I realize your list may be different:

1. Have your desk face a window that overlooks a scenic view. The room should have ample natural sunlight; this is why I don't like basement offices.

    I am high up on our third floor facing an oversize window that overlooks our heavily wooded back yard.
2. Treat yourself to a coffee maker for the office. I start every day with a couple of cups. I enjoy it and the caffeine helps start me up.
3. Have a refrigerator for cold drinks and snacks throughout the day to keep your energy up as needed.
4. See whether listening to music can make work more enjoyable; I have an extensive CD collection so I can tailor music to my work: classical for heavy thinking or rock to energize me.

5. If there is no one around to object, why not have your pet in your office with you? Our beloved golden retriever Princess would often relax on my office couch watching me work, until she passed away last weekend. She always put a smile on my face.

6. Wear the most comfortable clothes you can. In the winter for me it's usually a flannel shirt, slacks, and sneakers.

7. Maintain an optimum temperature for productivity in your office. For me that's room temperature — 68 degrees Fahrenheit — or a couple of degrees below.

A big priority in my life is having the ability to avoid doing things I do not want to do. Being self-employed gives me this ability to a degree having a conventional job did not.

6

SEVEN STEPS TO OUTRAGEOUS
BUSINESS SUCCESS

I spend a lot of time thinking about why some people are successful while others are not.

The reason for my doing so is probably the large number of people who e-mail me saying they are not successful and asking how they can become so.

On reflection, I think success is largely a matter of 7 factors coming into alignment:

1. Brains.

    Most of the successful people I know are smart — at least smart in business if not academically.

2. Talent.

    It helps if you can develop a specialized talent that the market is willing to pay for, such as designing computer systems or winning cases in court.

3. Aptitude.

   Some people naturally gravitate towards professions or activities that are lucrative; e.g. real estate investing. Others are attracted to activities that don't pay well; e.g. poetry.

4. Hard work.

   Most of the successful people I know don't just work smart; they also work hard — even though they may make proclamations to the contrary.

5. Persistence.

   Your chances of winning in the games of business and life increase exponentially if you are persistent and do not give up when faced with adversity, as so many do.

6. Luck.

   Let's face it: some of us get lucky while others don't. For instance, one exploration and production company strikes oil while another's well in the very same field comes up dry.

7. Timing.

   A lot of success is being in the right place at the right time. However, remember this observation from Pasteur: "Chance favors the prepared mind."

Also, you increase your odds of being in the right place at the right time by being in the right place all the time.

This is why successful entrepreneurs market continually rather than only when they need business: You never know when the perfect customer is going to go looking for what you sell, so the trick is to be there whenever they do look.

7

THE TROUBLE WITH ASKING STRANGERS FOR FAVORS

Last week, I got a heart-breaking e-mail from subscriber FG telling me all his woes and problems in life, which were considerable. Among them:

- He is bankrupt.
- He is behind in his mortgage and at risk for foreclosure.
- He had cancer.
- His younger son can't talk and is developmentally delayed.
- His older son had a nervous breakdown.

He then followed with a long list of all the things he wanted me to do for him — for free.

- Give him referrals (which I plan to do) for copywriting assignments I can't or don't want to handle.
- Outsource work to him (which I don't do).

- Help him get into the Internet marketing business (I am certainly happy to answer a brief question now and then, as I do for others).
- Refer clients to one of his clients, a marketing consultant (I don't have much interest in that, as I am a marketing consultant.)

As a compromise, I told him I could do a few of the favors, but not all of them ... I simply don't have the "bandwidth" (time) to provide the extensive assistance he requested, as much as I would want to.

I get an e-mail from a subscriber almost every week telling me sad tales — they are sick, they are broke, their kids are in jail — and asking me for free products, services, an endorsement, or other assistance to help them.

I am always sympathetic, and I think most people in my situation — those able to render assistance — are similarly sympathetic when someone in dire needs asks for help.

But what FG didn't know was that I had a list of troubles that could match his point by point:

- Hurricane Sandy had shut down my power, my PC, and my business for nearly a week in the midst of a crushing deadline.
- My mother was in Mexico last month, fell, and broke her hip. The doctor said flying was too dangerous so she had to have the surgery there, and then was too fragile to travel (she eventually got home).
- Last year my wife was diagnosed with stage IV ovarian cancer and I was told she had months to live. Fortunately, the diagnosis turned out to be wrong — she had lymphoma— but for a while we were living in a nightmare.
- My younger son called us 4am EST on a Thursday from Pittsburgh where he attends college to tell us he had pains in his abdomen so severe, he was taking himself to a hospital in an ambulance. Turns out he had appendicitis and needed immediate surgery. By the time we drove the 7 hours there, he had already had the operation.
- Princess, our beloved 9-year-old golden retriever, is having an MRI as I write this and may have a brain tumor.

What is the point of this rant about me and FG?

1. You may think you are the only one with problems or the one with the most serious problems. But everyone has problems, some as terrible — or more terrible — than yours.
2. It is OK to ask for help, and many people will give it, but there is usually a limit to how much help they can or will give you.
3. If someone you reach out to doesn't respond in the positive way you think they should, don't dwell on it. Move on. You have no idea of what they are dealing with right now. It would be nice — more humane — if they were more helpful. But remember, they don't owe you anything.

DO C-LEVEL EXECUTIVES
SPEAK A DIFFERENT LANGUAGE

I have dealt with this complaint before, but it comes up every now and then, and recently, I heard it from a potential client who wanted to sell Web services to marketing managers at Fortune 500 and middle market corporations.

"Our copy is too simple," the client said of his Web site. "This sounds as if we are talking to small business owners. Our audience is senior managers at Fortune 500 companies. The tone needs to be much more professional and sophisticated."

Oh, really? Says who?

One of the biggest misconceptions about writing to CEOs, CFOs, and other senior executives is that they speak some alien language that has only a passing resemblance to the conversational or written English you and I use every day ... and that, to sell to this special audience, you have to emulate or copy this special language.

But the reality is: C-level executives put their pants on one leg at a time just like everyone else. They read the same blogs you do … go to the same movies … listen to the same radio stations … watch the same TV shows.

Yes, it's smart marketing to understand your audience and then write copy that speaks to their specific needs, fears, concerns, problems, and desires.

And you want to tailor the tone and style of your language to your audience to a reasonable degree. For instance, you wouldn't use off-color language when writing to ministers. Or use equations in differential calculus when writing to factory workers.

But ministers, chemists, accountants, engineers, computer programmers, while they all may speak the specialized language of their trade, also speak a common language: the English language. And that's the language you should use when writing your copy.

How do I know I am right? The same way we know anything about direct marketing: through testing.

I have tested "plain English" copy against "high-falutin" copy numerous times over the span of my 34-year career in direct marketing … and 99 times out of 100, the same language that works for "ordinary folks" sells just as effectively to CEOs, Ph.D.s, and yes, even rocket scientists.

It is easy enough to see this for yourself. Study the controls in any market, for any kind of product. Collect as many e-mails and direct mail pieces as you can that you know to be strong controls, because they have been mailed repeatedly.

Now divide them into two piles: those written in plain English vs. those written in jargon, big words, or "high falutin" language. If you have collected a dozen samples, I guarantee that the number in the "plain English" pile will be 12 or 11 … no fewer than that … proving my point.

I once interviewed more than a hundred CEOs, including those at many Fortune 500 companies, to ghostwrite a book *Leadership Secrets of the World's Most Successful CEOs* (Dearborn). *Without exception*, they were all plain-speaking men and women, using direct, straightforward, conversational language in their written and oral communication — even those in computers and IT.

The world's most respected writing authorities all agree that good writing is clear, simple, and direct.

"Clutter is the disease of American writing," writes William Zinsser in *On Writing Well* (HarperCollins). "We are a society strangling in unnecessary words, circular constructions, pompous frills, and meaningless jargon."

And what about my claim that good writing is "conversational"?

"You can't actually write the way you talk," writes Rudolph Flesch in *The Art of Readable Writing* (Harper & Row). "You can, however, put a reasonable facsimile of your ordinary talking self on paper. You can purposely put into your writing certain things that will make it sound like talk." (He cites contractions as one example.)

One other point: as a chemical engineer myself, I have been writing copy aimed at engineers, scientists, mathematicians, systems analysts, and other "techies" for 34 years. And in all that time, I've never been told that the simple, plain English copy I wrote was "too easy to read."

Of course, you can always test my claim that plain English outpulls "high falutin" language for yourself. Here's how....

The next time a marketing manager says of your conversational copy, "It's not professional enough," offer to do a split test: your version against his.

Then you'll know definitively what works best for your audience ... rather than relying on his (or yours, or my) opinion.

(RG, a colleague, did this with a direct mail package aimed at executives, and his conversational version beat the "professional package" 3 to 1.)

Make sense? Of course. Doing an A/B split test always does, right?

ASKING PEOPLE FOR FREE ADVICE

At least once a day, I get an e-mail from a subscriber asking me to answer a question or provide an opinion.

A common one is: the subscriber sends me a link to her Web site. She then asks me to look at it and tell her what I think of it.

It seems like an innocent enough and reasonable request, right?

But here's why there's a problem with it:

First, I am constantly busy throughout the work day writing copy for my paying clients.

Clicking on the link to view the Web site is an interruption of my work, and I am always on deadline.

Plus, giving even a short critique of the site takes time I just don't have.

Second, Web site critiques are a service I offer on my web site www. bly.com, and I charge a modest fee for this service — far less than I charge for copywriting.

Yet my correspondents never acknowledge this, nor do they ever offer to pay for the opinion they are asking me to render.

Apparently either my time has no value or freelance writers are obliged to give away their work in a way that dentists, dry cleaners, and auto mechanics are not.

Another common situation is that a subscriber asks me a question, and the answer is fully articulated in one of my books.

In such cases, it would seem a reasonable suggestion on my part that they go out and get that book.

However, when I make this suggestion, some subscribers accuse me of being a profit-hungry, money-grubbing vulture preying on my readers by trying to sell them a $15 book.

In fact, many of my books and reports were written for the express purpose of answering the most commonly asked questions I get.

Since it would be impossible for me to write a personalized 5-page e-mail to everyone who asks the question, I figured by putting the answer in a book or report I would have a fast, efficient way of giving these folks a well thought out answer.

If you are an avid consumer of information products, you have most likely tried to correspond with some of your favorite gurus at one time or another, probably with mixed results.

Here are some tips that can help you communicate more effectively with the authors you read on a regular basis:

1. Most info product authors are busy people with a lot of projects and deadlines to contend with. Their time is limited and, to them, valuable. Respect it.

2. When asking for advice, tell the author you realize he is busy and may not have time to answer … but say you would appreciate it if they could.

3. Offer to pay the author his going rate for time. Many writers, including me, don't work with individuals and won't take your money. But it is nice for you to at least offer to pay me.

4. If the guru suggests you buy one of his information products, consider following his suggestion. Why should he spend uncompensated time with you when he has already thought through and written down the answer for you?

5. Don't write an e-mail of complaint when the author does not reply to your initial request in a timely manner. He is busy and has other priorities. Replying to your e-mail is not at the top of the list, although I do reply to all e-mails sent me.

6. If you plan on asking an author for advice on a regular basis, at least buy some of his books or other information products. I'm inclined to spend a little more time with someone who is a paying customer rather than with someone who reads my free e-mails but hasn't spent a dime with me.

10

FIND A NEED AND FILL IT.

The slaughter of 20 innocent children at an elementary school in Newton, CT has given birth to a chilling new product: a child's back pack with bullet-proof armor sewn into the lining.

The manufacturer of the bullet-proof back pack has simply followed the old marketing dictum of "find a need and fill it" ... though many might find their example abhorrent.

Nonetheless, "find a need and fill it" is good advice for us entrepreneurs looking to create products that sell.

Sy Sperling, founder and former president of the Hair Club for Men (HCM), found a need and filled it in his business: the need for bald men to have hair again.

Divorced at a relatively young age, Sy found himself single and thrust back into the dating scene.

But his hair loss made Mr. Sperling lose confidence in himself when hitting the clubs.

He looked at toupees. But these "rugs" were easy to spot and often ridiculed.

Then a relative took Sy to a hair salon that gave him a "weave" — a wig made of human hair that was somehow attached to the scalp, I think by weaving it into Sy's thinning remaining hair.

Sy saw a need to provide natural-looking hair to balding men who did not want to wear a rug … so he improved the design of the system for attaching the wig to the scalp and called it a "hair replacement system."

Sy was not instantly successful. There were problems with the early systems, which became easily tangled and matted when combed or wet.

Sy would come to his salon each morning to find men in the waiting area holding bags; the bags contained the tangled weaves that angry wives had cut off their heads.

Sy is credited as the inventor of the hair replacement industry, in which Hair Club for Men and Dr. Bosley are the biggest marketers, and he grew HCM to dozens of locations nationwide.

His famous line about HCM — "I'm not only the president; I'm also a client" — wasn't even written by Sy. His ad agency wrote that line. Jack Nicholson utters it in the movie Wolf when as a werewolf he begins to sprout new hair.

A few years ago, Sy sold HCM to a group of investors for $60 million. In a year or so, they turned around and sold it to another investor for over $200 million.

Sy is now a man of leisure living in a luxury condo in Boca Raton on the Atlantic Ocean.

If you have some down time during the holiday season, I recommend you spend some of it thinking about a need that exists out there that you could fill.

This brainstorming may lead to your most profitable product or business yet. It's certainly worth the effort.

11

ARE YOU A TYPE A OR TYPE B PERSONALITY?

Not too long ago, some TV commercials for Hardee's featuring ex-NYC police detective and millionaire entrepreneur Bo Dietl were aired.

I have a slight connection with this since I know Bo Dietl.

I coauthored a book with him about his business advice, "Business Lunchatations."

During one of our sessions, Bo said to me: "I am a type A personality. You are type B."

It was not an insult, but simply an observation — and an accurate one at that.

Bo is an aggressive, bold, hard-driving businessman ... a type A personality.

I am introverted, shy, retiring, even timid ... a type B personality.

What Bo and I have in common, although I never told him, is that we are both millionaires.

I tell you this not to brag but to let you know that you don't have to be a bold, driven type A personality — like Bo Dietl, Richard Branson, or Donald Trump — to make a good living or have a good career.

There is plenty of room in this world for us type B personalities.

Bo, for example, is the ultimate networker.

He told me he has business dinners in restaurants for networking virtually every night of the week.

I don't like networking, and there is almost never an evening that I don't spend at home with my family — and it's been that way for years.

Bo is a wheeler-dealer. He once got the contract to provide security for a major commercial building in NYC because he had Donald Trump on his personal speed-dialer, and Trump vouched for him.

Bo is a meticulous dresser, always perfectly groomed and wearing thousand-dollar suits.

I own one $200 suit and I wear it, against my will, a handful of times a year. Since I work at home and clients never see me, I luxuriate in the habit of shaving sporadically.

Many superstar entrepreneurs and executives of fame are type As, including Mark Cuban, Larry Ellison, and Simon Cowell.

I don't know, but I suspect, that some others may be type Bs — Larry Page, Mark Zuckerberg, Bill Gates.

More often, us type Bs run smaller businesses that fly under the public radar. We don't own private jets or private islands like Ellison. We don't make the Forbes 500 richest people list. But many of us earn handsome livings and live comfortable lives from our entrepreneurial efforts.

My point — and I do have one — is that you don't have to feel guilty if you aren't a hard-driving type A personality.

Don't look at all those rich and famous type As and boil with envy. You can do fine in life the way you are.

As a young person, I felt constant guilt that I wasn't a wealthy jet-setting tycoon driving a Rolls Royce. It gave me an inferiority complex.

Now, more mature at 55, I am comfortable with who and what I am, and what I have achieved … and although I could buy a Rolls Royce today, I prefer my Toyota Prius with its hybrid engine and 45 mpg.

Don't worry so much about trying to be like your rich and famous role models. Just be the best you you can be.

As Jerry Lewis says in The Nutty Professor, "If you don't like yourself, how do you expect others to?"

12

THREE WAYS TO WIN
AT E-MAIL MARKETING

Today I want to share with you the three most important things I've learned about writing winning e-mail marketing campaigns.

- The first is: when your e-mail copy makes reference to what's going on in the news the same week — or even better, the same day — you distribute it, your response rates soar.

Financial publishers were probably the first to discover this: e-mail messages that reflect what's going on in the market on the day they are distributed — for instance, "gold hits $1,700 per ounce … should you sell or buy more?" — pull much better than generic promotional e-mails or those with evergreen content.

The idea of including news in your copy is not new. But e-mail marketing makes it easier to more precisely coordinate and time your e-mail messages with current events and developments.

Of course, it is easier to tie in with news and current events for some products than others. A company that sells aluminum siding to homeowners might find it more difficult to link their e-mail copy to Obama's latest speech than a company promoting oil and gas stocks.

But it's not impossible. And any time your e-mail can reflect news or trends, readership and response are likely to soar.

- My second tip for writing winning e-mail messages: giving away content in the e-mail itself is, contrary to what you might expect, a way to strengthen copy and results.

I say "contrary to what you might expect" because, you might reason, "If I give the information away in the e-mail, the reader's curiosity is satisfied, and he does not have to click through to find the answers he is looking for."

The trick is to give "partial content" — as a sample of the kind of help your product, service, or firm offers.

Ideally, this could be something as quick as a simple how-to tip embedded in the e-mail copy. Then, you promise many more useful tips and advice when the reader clicks through.

This works for two reasons. First, people are trained on the Internet to expect free content, so this technique fulfills their expectation.

Second, including actual content in your e-mail marketing — and not just teasing the reader with promises to provide valuable content when they respond — demonstrates your expertise and knowledge right then and there in the e-mail.

The reader is quickly convinced you know what you are talking about — and therefore, may be a resource he wants to know better.

- My third tip for writing winning e-mail messages: open rates and click-through rates both increase when your e-mail marketing messages match — in look, content, tone, and style — the other e-mails prospects get from you or the list owner on a regular basis.

For instance, if your e-mail is going to an opt-in list of subscribers to a text e-newsletter, your response will be better if you send a text e-mail rather than an HTML.

If people on your list are used to extremely short e-mail messages, a long-copy e-mail blast probably won't work as well as a short teaser e-mail linked to a landing page where they can read the rest of your message.

Take a look at past e-mail promotions to the list that worked as well as issues of e-newsletters these readers receive.

If they all contain graphs ... or technical information ... or pictures of pets ... or news ... or a pithy how-to tip ... or survey results ... then your e-mail probably should, too.

Reason: people on a given list are "trained" to accept e-mails with similar look and feel to the ones they get regularly.

When your e-mail matches their expectations, they believe it's something they read regularly and open it.

When your e-mail looks wildly different, they view it as spam and delete.

13

WHAT'S WORKING IN DIRECT MAIL TODAY

In his book *Secrets of Successful Direct Mail* (Bottom Line Books), the late mail order consultant Dick Benson says: "Self-mailers almost never work."

"Testing has consistently proven a one-page letter with a compelling offer outperforms a glossy mailer [in business-to-business lead generation] by 100 percent," says Liz Taylor of Liz Taylor Marketing.

And in an issue of his e-newsletter, copywriter Alan Sharpe says, "In business-to-business direct mail lead generation, letters invariably outpull self-mailers, including postcards."

As a copywriter, I've always been prejudiced in favor of sales letters, because it's my favorite form to write.

But obviously, a sales letter is not always better than a postcard or other self-mailer — and in recent years, I've come to love postcards for the results they can produce for marketers on a budget.

Consider subscription promotion for magazines, where double postcards and vouchers routinely outperform traditional letter packages on an ROI basis.

For more than a decade, Medical Economics tested all sorts of letter packages against a snap-pack control for Physician's Desk Reference. None of them could beat the self-mailer.

And look at the outrageous success of the magalog — a long-copy self-mailer format — in selling nutritional supplements and consumer newsletters.

The copywriters I talked to were split. A few, like Ivan Levison and Herschell Gordon Lewis, praised self-mailers and said they can work well. Others, such as Sharpe and Jeffrey Dobkin, are clearly fans of sales letters.

"On a dollar-for-dollar basis, self-mailers can outperform a closed-face envelope in b-to-b mailings," says copywriter Herschell Gordon Lewis.

"No, you can't get mailed credit card information. But more and more, when the pitch is for a phone call or online response, a quick look gets read where a classic mailing seems ponderous.

"Closed-face means either a two-way match-up or an unimprinted response device, both of which kick costs upward. Windows scream, 'This is a bulk mailing.'"

"The great advantage of the self-mailer is that it's cheap," says Ivan Levison, a copywriter specializing in software. "It's also easy for the prospect to unfold a self-mailer. There's no envelope to tear open, so you know that you stand a good chance of getting the reader into your message.

"The self-mailer is a good choice for making noisy announcements, which is why retailers use them at sales time. If you have a simple, clear story to tell, a self-mailer can make a great deal of sense."

A lot of copywriters, ad agencies, and marketing consultants like packages better than self-mailers because they can charge the client more for them, and because they find writing and designing letter packages more fun and rewarding creatively. Not a good reason to use them, of course, as Jeffrey Dobkin admits.

"When clients ask me what is the most effective piece we can send I always say a letter," says Dobkin. "And it's not just because letters are my specialty or that I charge so much for them. I do think letters are the most effective you can be with the understanding that this is in most instances. There are exceptions.

"A personal-looking letter is almost always opened. I like the teaser 'Gift Certificate Enclosed' on anything that looks commercial: the open rate is exceptional."

"In certain situations, letters may outperform self-mailers," says copywriter Joan Damico. "In business-to-business direct mail, getting through the corporate mail room may be better served with a #10 letter package.

"It also depends on what stage in the buying cycle the prospect is receiving the mailing. A prospect in the awareness phase may respond better to a colorful self-mailer, while a customer in the loyalty phase may respond better to a #10 letter package."

Here are a few rules of thumb that can help you select the right format — traditional letter package, self-mailer, or postcard — for your next mailing:

- Postcards can work well when the primary response you seek is a visit to a Web URL or a call to your toll-free number.
- When your story is detailed and complex, a traditional letter package is likely to work best.
- Study your market. See what formats are being used in your competitors' controls. Use the same formats for your mailings — at least to begin with.

Of course, the ultimate strategy for format selection is to split test — and let consumers vote with their responses.

14

BIGGEST SELF-HELP
MYTH EXPOSED

Self-help gurus and motivational speakers love to tell us that whatever we want, we can do, have, or become.

Napoleon Hill said, "Whatever the mind can conceive and believe, it can achieve."

Earl Nightingale: "Whatever we plant in our subconscious mind and nourish with repetition and emotion will one day become a reality."

The problem with this is: it's not always true.

Examples:

- Unless you have a high IQ, you can't become an astrophysicist.
- Unless you are athletic, you won't get drafted by the Patriots.
- Unless you can sing, you probably won't win American Idol and get a record deal.

What many positive thinkers ignore is that it takes more than just positive thoughts to achieve a goal.

And here's what it does take to do or become what you desire:

- First, you need the equipment: the aptitude, affinity, and knack for a particular field or profession.

   Example: I am 56, short, dumpy, and nonathletic. I would like to be the Jets quarterback. But no matter what I think, it isn't going to happen.

   But I do have an affinity for teaching. So I have routinely been paid thousands of dollars a day to give training classes and seminars.

- Second, you need desire.

   This is especially true in fields like acting, music and sports where competition for a limited number of opportunities is incredibly fierce.

   Unless you have a burning desire for the goal, you won't stick with it and make the effort it takes to get there.

- Third, you must be persistent.

   The old adage: If at first you don't succeed, try, try again.

   Winston Churchill: "Never give up."

   In my observation, most people who want to pursue an accomplishment or achievement give up way too early.

- Fourth, talent.

   You should have some natural talent or, if not, enormous enthusiasm for the field in which you want to make your mark.

   If you are not naturally talented, you can develop many of the skills you need (e.g. Web site design) through practice and study.

- Fifth, skill.

   In today's competitive world, it's tough to make a go of things if you are poor or mediocre in your profession.

   To increase the odds of success in your favor, you must get really good at what you do. The key is: practice.

Mark Ford says you can get good at just about anything by doing it for a thousand hours ... and become a master when you have done it ten thousand hours.

- Sixth, training.

Your training may be on the job or in the classroom. It could be night school, seminars, in-house courses offered by your company, or college.

But you must acquire the basic knowledge practitioners in your field are expected to have.

As a copywriter since 1979, I knew how to write.

But when SEO become a discipline some years ago, I took a Direct Marketing Association self-study course to learn it.

- Seventh, you need connections.

Very few people realize their dreams entirely on their own.

Cultivating a network of colleagues, specialists, and potential clients or employers can give you an enviable shortcut to your goal.

15

FAIL YOUR WAY TO SUCCESS.

In most of the things I've done in my writing career, I've failed.

For example, I have written numerous short stories and submitted them to magazines that publish fiction.

I haven't sold a single one. I could wallpaper our bathroom with the rejection slips.

I've made several significant false starts at a novel, but never could come up with a story idea I felt could sustain a novel-length work.

So ... no novel published.

I have sent queries for articles to magazines like my beloved New York Review of Books, but the only major consumer magazine to publish my work was Cosmopolitan.

(And I didn't even write an original article for Cosmo; they reprinted a chapter from one of my career books.)

Similarly, I have never published a poem ... sold a screenplay ... or even gotten paid to write a greeting card. (My mother — a nonwriter — did write and get paid for several greeting cards. Can you believe it?)

In my youth I dreamed of being a newspaper reporter, but no newspaper would hire me, and I sent resumes to 300 newspaper editors.

Yet despite ongoing, massive failure in a wide spectrum of the writing profession, I make a good living as a full-time freelance writer and am quite happy doing it.

The secret is that there are a couple of areas of writing where I have been at least reasonably successful.

The main ones are freelance copywriting and as a nonfiction book author, with 80 books published by mainstream publishing houses.

I have also had some success marketing information products on the Internet.

Just a few hits among the many misses — yet the few writing activities I succeed at have earned me literally millions of dollars over the decades.

My point — and I do have one — is that you don't have to be successful at everything you try ... or even at most things you try ... to have a great career and a great life.

GB, a colleague, had wanted to write for the theater, but never had a play published or produced.

Now GB makes thousands of dollars a day teaching business writing to managers and support staff for corporate clients.

He paints — very good abstracts — as an avocation. GB will never earn a living as an artist. But he recently had a show at a local gallery.

When I was in college, I dreamed of writing the Great American Novel ... not the Great American Sales Letter.

But sales letters are what I write today, online and offline. It's loads of fun for me — and the pay is attractive.

If you haven't hit it big in writing, Internet marketing, or whatever your area of interest is, could it be that you simply haven't discovered your "sweet spot" yet — the one area to which you are naturally suited and are likely to thrive in?

My late colleague, GR, had little success in writing magazine and newspaper ads, though he was enthralled with advertising and wanted to write it.

But then GR got an assignment to write a radio commercial, and lightning struck!

He loved writing the radio spot, the client loved the copy, and he began a successful career as a freelance radio commercial writer that lasted for decades.

If you feel your career or business is stalled, try new things in different areas of your niche that you haven't explored yet.

The more things you try — and in writing, I've tried a lot of them — the better your chances of hitting your sweet spot ... and finding success and happiness in your profession.

To quote Winston Churchill: Never give up!

16

WRITE LIKE YOUR READER TALKS.

We copywriters are taught to write conversational copy. Many marketers erroneously think "conversational copy" means "write like you talk."

But what it really means is "write the way your prospects talk."

A public radio station in my area, featuring eclectic rock and pop, sent me a fundraising letter. It began: "Dear Neighbor: I know you are a savvy media consumer."

Now, I don't know about you, but if you ask me why I listen to the radio, I would not say because I am a savvy media consumer; I'd say, "I like music."

Here's my rewrite for the fundraising letter lead:

"Dear Fellow Music Lover: Do you ever wish, when you turn on the radio, that they'd play OUR music?"

While my rewrite hasn't been tested against the original, I believe it's an improvement, for two reasons.

First, it talks about something the reader cares about: hearing music I like when I turn on the radio.

Second, it establishes an empathy-based bond through a common interest between the reader and the writer: that we share similar musical tastes — which is why I said "our" music instead of "your" music.

"In most cases, you should write in a conversational, intimate voice," says copywriter Susanna K. Hutcheson. "You should talk as if you're having coffee with the reader and use her language.

"Many copywriters, and just about all people who write their own copy, don't understand the concept of writing in the language of the reader. It's truly an art."

Is there any situation where you should use language other than conversational copy? What about writing to sophisticated audiences? Don't specialists prefer jargon when discussing their industry or trade?

Some argue that jargon is appropriate because it's language used by specialists in your target audience. But I think they confuse jargon with technical terms.

Technical terms are words or phrases that communicate a concept or idea more precisely and concisely than ordinary terms. Example: "operating system" to describe the software that controls the basic operations of a computer.

Jargon, on the other hand, is language more complex than the ideas it serves to communicate.

Example: I worked for a company that made industrial equipment.

In one of our products, a door opened at the bottom of a silo, allowing powder to fall into a dump truck underneath. Our chief engineer insisted that in our copy we replace "dumped" with "gravimetrically conveyed."

For a client, I wrote that the dental brace they manufactured helped keep loose teeth in place. The product manager rewrote "keep loose teeth in place" to "stabilize mobile dentition."

To me, this is like calling the sea shore an "ocean-land interface."

Mark Twain said "I never write metropolis when I get paid the same amount of money to write the word city."

But is there an exception to the rule of writing the way people talk? A situation where you would deliberately use language more complex than the idea it serves to communicate?

Yes, and the one case in which you might consider replacing ordinary language with more sophisticated phraseology is when you want to set your product above the ordinary.

Take a look at a Mont Blanc catalog. They don't describe their products as pens; they sell "writing instruments."

Why? Because Mont Blanc pens start at about $100 … and, while that's too much to pay for a pen, it's not too much to pay for a "writing instrument."

The goal of direct response copywriting is not to produce perfect prose or great writing. It is to persuade the consumer to buy your product.

And the bottom line is: the copywriter should do whatever it takes to achieve that goal, whether or not writing purists approve.

For instance, grammarians dislike the phrase "free gift," complaining that "free" is inherent in the definition of gift: what gift isn't free? But in a recent lecture, my colleague Herschell Gordon Lewis defended "free gift" because it works, explaining that "each word reinforces the other."

I remember years ago hearing about a mailer who actually split test "free gift" vs. "gift." Not only did "free gift" win handily, but a number of recipients of the "gift" letter responded by inquiring to ask whether the gift was indeed free.

Which reminds me of what Ralph Waldo Emerson once said: "It is not enough to write so you can be understood; you must write so clearly that you cannot be misunderstood."

17

THE TIME FOR ACTION IS NOW.

The Wednesday before Thanksgiving, my garage door wouldn't open.

So I called the service that installed the door opener and asked them to fix it.

TR, the technician they send, is normally chatty. But on Wednesday he was subdued.

He asked me how I had made out during Hurricane Sandy, and I told him about our power being out for a week.

"How did you do?" I asked.

Turns out — not so good.

A tree fell through the front of his father-in-law's house.

A limb impaled his father-in-law, instantly killing the man.

TR's wife was standing next to her dad when he died.

Why am I telling you this?

It occurs to me that a lot of people who contact me for help act as if they have all the time in the world to pursue their dreams.

Whether it's becoming a freelance copywriter or starting an Internet marketing business, they have a seemingly endless list of excuses why they haven't taken the leap yet — and can't for some time.

But as TR's father-in-law sadly discovered, we don't have infinite time.

Life is very short. If you are over 50, like me, your life is likely more than half over.

I used to believe in the excuses and accept procrastination.

"I have to stay in my job until I get my raise," one subscriber told me.

There was a time I thought that made good sense. Now I think it is a wasteful delay.

Nike has it right. If you want to do something, "just do it."

Don't wait until you attend that one more webinar ... or take that one more course ... or read that classic marketing book ... or learn PowerPoint ... or furnish your spare bedroom as a home office.

The time to pursue your dream is now.

Lots of people tell me they can't start their new business because they don't know enough about marketing yet.

Well, doing something — not just reading about it — is the best way to learn it.

When I started my career as a freelance copywriter, I had only a couple of years of copywriting experience ... yet somehow, I managed to succeed.

Back then, I had a mentor, SR, who recently passed away.

When I was contemplating becoming a freelance copywriter, I told SR that maybe I would get a job with a direct response ad agency for a few years to gain some experience.

"That's a waste of some good years," SR replied. "If you want to be a freelance copywriter, be a freelance copywriter."

My colleague Mark Ford expresses it this way: "Ready. Fire. Aim."

He says that people spending too much time planning and preparing, when they should be doing.

If you have ever contacted me and told me why you haven't started your freelance or entrepreneurial career yet, make a New Year's Resolution to tell me — next time you e-mail me — that you HAVE started your new career or business.

I assure you that will make both of us happy.

18

MAKE YOURSELF INDISPENSABLE.

While he was alive, Robert B. Parker was my favorite suspense writer.

He wrote a series of novels featuring a wise-cracking private eye named Spencer.

Recently his publisher released a new Spencer novel, even though Parker died a few years ago.

It was not a manuscript Parker left behind.

The publisher hired suspense writer Ace Atkins to take over the Spencer series.

I read the book and grudgingly have to admit that it is so good that it reads as if Parker wrote it.

That means new Spencer novels will keep coming out even though the creator is gone.

My point — and I do have one — is that almost no one is indispensable.

That's a problem, because the more dispensable you are, the more readily you can be fired from your job.

Almost no one is truly indispensable. Even a great employee can be fired at the whim of her employer.

But if you are currently an employee, there are really only 3 ways to make yourself less dispensable.

1. Generate revenue or cost savings in excess of your salary.

    Employees who generate a positive ROI (return on investment) on their compensation are usually the last to be let go.
2. Offer a service or skill not readily available elsewhere in your organization.

    Technical specialists often have more job security than managers. (With outsourcing, this is less true for IT professionals.)
3. Start and run your own business.

    When you are your own boss, you can't be fired.

However, your customers can abandon you to buy from your competitors, if they choose to do so.

Here are a few ways to keep customers satisfied and prevent loss of business:

- Don't be the low-priced service provider. Always being the low bid creates the perception that your service must be inferior. Exceptions? Of course.
- Set your prices in the middle of the top third of the price range for your category of service. This ensures a good profit margin but avoids being priced so high that buyers hesitate to hire you.
- Pick an underserved niche in your market to specialize in. The lack of competition can make you close to indispensable to many clients.
- Always provide exceptional customer service. Never give a customer a reason to question their relationship with you.
- Always provide added value, so that the price you charge seems like a drop in the bucket compared to the value you deliver.

- Find a metric that can be measured to demonstrate how your service makes the client more money, saves money, saves time, or otherwise produces a positive ROI.

The most indispensable business I've ever seen was my local Lowes right after hurricane Sandy.

They had customers lined up around the block hoping to buy a portable gasoline-powered generator before they ran out.

I can tell you from personal experience that if you don't own a generator and the lights go out, you will do almost anything to get one.

If you and I figure out how to package our services so they are as indispensable as a generator in a power outage, we'll be rich I tell you — rich!

19

HAVE AN ATTITUDE OF GRATITUDE

I used to be a complainer and even a whiner ... but thanks in part to Hurricane Sandy I don't think I will be any more.

I'm the guy who, when he gets a flat tire, kicks the car, curses, and bemoans his fate — rather than just calling AAA or getting the jack out and changing the tire.

A few weeks back, I got ticked off because the ice cube dispenser on the refrigerator door didn't work. (What a baby!)

A month ago, someone hacked all my Web sites. I had steam coming out of my ears.

But look at the devastation of hurricane Sandy. Many homes here in NJ were destroyed. Others were so damaged the residents had to move to a shelter.

Here we dodged a bullet. During the height of the storm Monday night, we lost power, huge branches came down in our tree-filled yard, and screen windows flew off the house.

A tall, skinny tree on the front lawn bent like blade of grass in the wind, and we were certain it would hit the house. Again, we were lucky. But we are going to have that tree removed.

Now in NJ we have gas rationing. I have almost no gas in my car, which means I can't drive any significant distance. The gas lines easily have 2-3 hour waits, something for which I have neither time nor patience.

The news says this will ease up soon, and I am waiting for that. Fortunately, working at home, I don't have to drive to work or go anywhere else.

Hurricane Sandy serves as a reminder to me that we shouldn't sweat the small stuff, because there are really bad things that can happen to you — things that most of us are lucky enough to dodge — but some aren't.

Readers call or e-mail me all the time with their business problems. For instance, a promotion they ran failed to get the results they expected. Or a client gave them a hard time.

I don't mean to minimize these problems. They can be painful.

But my new attitude is: any day you wake up in good health with a roof over your head and food to eat is a good day.

This attitude of gratitude has already brought me some peace and contentment. It may do the same for you too.

20

KEEP YOUR PC RUNNING
IN ANY SITUATION.

This may be the most important tip I give you this year, and not one person in a hundred is aware of it:

If you use a gasoline generator when your power goes out, do NOT hook up your PC to it.

Gasoline generators produce "dirty" power, meaning it fluctuates in voltage to a level unacceptable to a PC's sensitive circuitry.

My PC guy said that after hurricane Sandy, he had 25 clients with PC problems, all of whom connected their computers to a gasoline generator — including me.

I was lucky: he got my computer back online in a few hours, and the only damage was to my back-up drive.

Every other client had severe damage, from destruction of the PC motherboard to complete loss of data on their hard drives.

The reason I wasn't wiped out is that the subpar current from our gasoline generator did not allow my PC to operate steadily, so I couldn't even use it. Turns out this was lucky for me, because I then disconnected the generator.

If you lose power during a storm or for any other reason, do not under any circumstance connect your computer to your back-up gasoline generator. You risk destruction of your PC and loss of all your data.

Here in NJ, we got hit hard by hurricane Sandy. We lost power, Internet, cable TV, heat, and hot water for nearly a week. The power outage shut down my business for the week.

Our home phones didn't work, but fortunately my office phone is with another carrier and it did.

There are worse things than losing power for a week, but it certainly ranks up there.

Our gas generator produces sufficient power to run appliances other than computers, so we connected our refrigerator to it and our food didn't spoil.

Without TV and Internet, you feel alone in the dark, not knowing the status of the storm. Fortunately we could plug in my little boom box to the generator and keep up that way.

(Without a generator, we wouldn't have even had the radio. There had been a run on D batteries, and they were impossible to get.)

Many others in NJ were not so lucky: we saw a long line of people at Lowe's hoping there would be enough generators to go around.

Even with a gas generator, your power is not assured, because what can you do when you can't get gasoline? Most gas stations had either run out of gas or had no power to pump the gas they had.

To conserve gasoline, we ran the generator intermittently. At night, we could see by candle light, and we hung out in front of a roaring fire.

We are now getting quotes for a full-house, natural-gas-fired generator. I want to make sure my business is never affected by a power outage ever again.

Some scientists predict these super storms will happen with increased frequency. Our experience supports that. We used to get one big storm here every 10 years. Now it seems to be an annual occurrence.

I also learned something about me: if I can't work and write every day, I become restless and jumpy. I am only relaxed and happy when I write every day.

21

STOP BRAGGING.

As a short person, I am sensitive to the fact that many big and tall men are unduly proud of being big and tall.

"Well, I'm a big guy," one said to me nonchalantly.

"I'm like a big old bear," said another tall guy proudly, this one with a shaggy head of hair and a beard.

Smart people are the same way: unduly proud of being so smart.

Beautiful or handsome people — same story.

Well guess what?

You shouldn't be proud of being big or tall or handsome or beautiful or smart.

That's because you didn't do anything to earn these attributes.

They are the results of genetics — and for intelligence, also the environment you were raised in.

So don't brag about being tall — you did nothing to earn it.

So what should you brag about?

You could brag about what you have accomplished using those attributes.

A tall man makes the basketball team ... a beautiful woman becomes a model ... a smart person earns a Ph.D.

But actually, it's unseemly to brag about even these accomplishments — because bragging itself is unseemly.

If someone asks about an accomplishment (e.g., what's your bowling average), you answer.

But if you are not asked, don't volunteer it.

Telling someone about your attributes and accomplishments without being asked to is boasting, pure and simple.

It's not an attractive personality trait. Many people are repelled by it. "Nobody likes a braggart" is an old observation.

To paraphrase Shakespeare, neither a braggart nor a boaster be.

22

STICK TO YOUR NICHE.

Recently, I have been getting a spate of e-mails from Red Lobster inviting me to eat there.

Based on the heavy frequency, I suspect they are spam, though I may be wrong.

Either way, they are reaching the wrong audience with me, because — odd though it may be — I don't like lobster.

I have no patience with cracking the shell to get the meat.

I figure that any creature bothering to evolve armor to keep me out deserves to be left alone.

Also the texture and taste don't do much for me.

If you are an Internet information marketer, you can't afford, like Red Lobster, to send e-mails to people without demonstrated interest in your niche.

Reason: the response rate will be unprofitable and people on your list will be offended and opt out.

I know this because I tested it once.

I created an e-book, all from public domain information, called Cheap Car Tips and Tricks — showing you how to save money on everything from repairs to gas. You can see the landing page here:

http://www.cheapcartips.com/

I then did an e-mail blast to my list. We sold maybe 3 copies.

In addition, we got e-mails in response that said things like:

"Bob, I subscribe to your e-mails for marketing tips, not car information. What do you know about cars anyway?"

I have seen repeatedly that the better targeted a product is to the interests of my subscribers, the more sales I will make.

Conversely, when I do an affiliate deal for a product I like (say a book on leadership written by a colleague) but that is not 100% focused on marketing or entrepreneurship, sales are mediocre at best.

You may be thinking: "Duh, Bob. This isn't exactly rocket science. It's painfully obvious, even to a dolt like you."

Maybe. But I see this rule violated every day.

I also get requests from people all the time asking me to promote the stuff to my list that my subscribers would have no possible interest in — ranging from vitamins to children's books.

If you want to be successful as an Internet information marketer, focus your content and product offers with laser-like intensity on your specialty topic — the topic that got people to subscribe to your list in the first place.

That is a key to making money online.

In the meantime: Anybody out there want to buy a book on cars from me?

TWENTY ONE THINGS THAT ARE WRONG ABOUT MODERN MARKETING.

Here are 21 things I don't like about modern marketing:

1. Telemarketing calls from a robot.
2. Telemarketing calls from a telemarketer.
3. A direct mailer that is a challenge just to open.
4. Freelance writers who call themselves "content strategists.
5. Having to make a separate version of Web sites and e-mails for smart phones.
6. Ads that allow you to respond only by scanning a QR code and have no phone number or other response mechanism.
7. People whom I don't even know inviting me to be their Facebook friend.
8. Online videos or audios that start as soon as you open a Web page without giving me the option of choosing whether I want to view or hear it.

9. TV commercials from local business owners with the production values of a bad elementary school play.

10. Hype-filled long-copy landing pages where the marketer brags endlessly about how rich and successful he is.

11. Marketers who offer free tapes or other freebies in their advertising and then don't send them — because they are doing a bait and switch.

12. Print ads with type that is 10 point or smaller.

13. Print ads and Web sites with type that is approximately the same color as the background.

14. Body copy in reverse type (white on a black or other dark background).

15. Dynamic Web copy that rotates before you have a chance to read it.

16. Branding consultants who advise clients that long copy doesn't work.

17. Social media consultants who act as if social networking is the most powerful marketing medium in the world.

18. Graphic designers who think the design is more important than the words.

19. Marketers who don't have an offer in their marketing.

20. Marketers who don't have a USP in their marketing.

21. Marketers who haven't read Hopkins, Caples, Ogilvy, Collier, Schwab, Sackheim, or Reeves — and in fact have never heard of them. Yikes!

24

DO WHAT MAKES YOU HAPPY.

This past weekend, my wife and eldest son and I went to a beautiful little stable in Pennsylvania so we could ride horses.

Well, they rode the horses. I declined.

The truth is I am not crazy about horses. They bite and kick and horse stables smell pretty bad.

Also, whenever I am on a horse, it never does what I tell it to.

So while they rode for an hour, I sat outside at a picnic table and read my favorite publication, the New York Review of Books.

It was a beautiful autumn day. I was surrounded by hills with an explosion of trees decorated green, brown, yellow, orange, and red.

After the ride, my wife and son told me, "You really missed out on all the fun."

But I didn't.

I did what I wanted to do and I really enjoyed myself.

My point — and I do have one — is that you shouldn't do what others think you should do just to make them happy.

You should do what you want to do to make yourself happy.

When I graduated from college, I took a corporate job which pleased my father to no end.

In his mind it paid a steady salary and was safe and secure.

But I was bored. So I became a freelance writer.

He felt I was making a mistake, giving up my safe and secure corporate job and my steady salary.

Early on in my freelancing, I did a large job for a software company and got a check for $10,000. (This was a lot of money in the early 1980s).

Wisely, I photocopied the check and showed it to my father.

After he put his eyes back in his head, he never complained about me quitting my corporate job ever again.

Make yourself happy. When you do, those who care about you will eventually be happy for you.

And if they're not, well — that's too bad for them.

25

HOW TO GET PEOPLE
TO TRUST YOU

MA, one of my subscribers, recently wrote to me.

He said, "These days, trust is the ultimate Unique Selling Proposition."

And in their book *Creating Trust*, Matt Zagula and Dan Kennedy state: "Trust is the pre-requisite for obtaining clients, opening accounts, client retention, and referrals."

Trust is especially difficult to build in Internet marketing, where consumers perceive that many of the marketers are con men and hucksters.

Here are some things I do in my Internet information marketing business that I hope build my subscribers' trust in me:

1. I promptly honor all requests for refunds.
2. Even if the customer requests a refund a few days or a few weeks after the 90-day deadline has passed, we still give her the refund.
3. I keep my product prices fair and modest, so prospects do not feel I am trying to squeeze every last dollar out of them.

4. We respond to all e-mails. If it's a marketing question, I answer it personally. If it involves a refund, product defect, or other product issue, my assistant Jodi handles it.

5. I am easy to get in contact with, unlike many other Internet marketers. For example, I pick up my own phone.

6. My products are accurate as far as I know. Not because I know everything, but because I only write or record information products on topics I have first-hand experience with.

7. My writing reflects my personality. Subscribers feel they have gotten to know me, and you are more likely to buy from someone you know than someone you don't.

8. My e-mails and Web sites are purposefully low key. The more you use hype in your copy, the less people trust you.

9. I don't brag endlessly to readers about my money or my houses or my cars or our vacations. People dislike braggarts.

10. I do not have a big ego. This too endears me to subscribers.

11. I give away a lot of valuable free content in my e-mails and on my various Web sites. Some of it you can get even without giving me your e-mail address.

12. I have written 80 books published by trade publishers. This credential validates me as an expert in the eyes of some readers.

13. I have 34 years experience in marketing. My longevity reassures some people that I know what I am doing.

14. I am 55 years old. My gray hairs are a comfort for baby boomers and mature adults who are distrustful of the very young and inexperienced.

15. I have an enormous collection of testimonials on my Web site: http://www.bly.com/newsite/Pages/Testimonials.html

26

WHY INFORMATION PRODUCTS ARE LIKE FRUIT.

When you guys have a complaint, I listen.

And you've been loud and clear lately about one thing: the need for me to update my information products.

There's a lesson here for both of us regarding the Internet information marketing business.

The lesson is that information products are like fruit.

They start out sweet and crisp, full of juicy content.

But they begin to spoil with age.

Eventually, they get rotten, and have to be replaced (or in the case of an info product, at least updated).

This was not so much the case in the pre-Internet, pre-e-book era.

Back then, we went to the public library, and did our research with the books and periodicals on hand.

We thought nothing of using a book that was 3 ... 5 ... even 10 years old.

We were just happy to have found a book containing the information we needed!

Today, it's different.

Things are changing at such a rapid rate, an e-book I published 4 years ago may already be out of date.

Actually, it depends on the topic.

With a topic like Internet marketing, the techniques used evolve so rapidly, products need to be updated every few years.

With a topic like time management, it's more of an "evergreen." The principles don't change, and a book written on time management in 1960 is probably 90% relevant to today.

Yet you can still make a case for a revised edition to encompass today's new time-saving technologies like smart-phones.

So why am I telling you this?

For two reasons:

First, if you are an info marketer, this is a clarion call to get off your butt, go through all your products, and start updating the ones that are dated.

Second, I want you to know that I am doing this very thing: going through all my products and making plans for updates.

We just updated two of our most popular products, the Internet Marketing Retirement Plan (www.theinternetmarketingretirementplan.com) and Online Research (www.fastonlineresearch.com).

Plans for updating another dozen are in the works. We will announce each update via e-mail to you when ready.

The point is: you have to listen to your customers and give them what they want.

You guys told me my products are starting to "age out." I heard you, and we are doing something about it to bring you the most current, useful marketing strategies.

End of commercial.

Action steps for you:

1. Ask your customers what they want if they are not already telling you ... and act on what they ask for.
2. Monitor your info products to make sure they are current and update or replace the ones that are not.

27

SHOULD YOUR WORRY ABOUT INTERNET PIRACY?

Subscriber SS asks me, "How do I prevent e-book pirating?

Here are my thoughts on the subject....

To begin with, I see too many folks focusing on e-book pirating — when instead they should be focusing on how to sell their e-book.

That's far more important and the biggest challenge. You've written an e-book. But how do you let readers know about it so they can buy?

I have been writing and publishing e-books since November 2004, and e-book pirating has never been a problem or much of a concern to me.

That being said, there are a few things you can do to foil the Internet pirates.

- Put a full-page in your e-book talking about a fantastic bonus that you offer only to buyers of that e-book. You only give the bonus to registered owners.

If someone has a pirated copy, you offer to sell them a legal copy which then entitles them to the free bonus.

- Put URLs for the landing pages of your other products throughout the e-book or on one page at the beginning or the end.

That way, the pirate is essentially distributing an online sales brochure for your other products free for you.

- Put the copyright symbol (i.e. © 2010) on a separate copyright page that appears right after the front cover.

- Register the copyright for your e-book at the U.S. copyright office in Washington DC.

- Add this text to the copyright page: "No portion of this e-book may be reprinted or reproduced in any way without the author's express written permission except by the authorized purchaser of the e-book."

- Also add this warning in a box: "This is not a free e-book. Purchase of this e-book entitles the buyer to keep one copy on his or her computer and to print out one copy only.

"Printing out more than one copy — or distributing it electronically — is prohibited by international and U.S.A copyright laws and treaties, and would subject the purchaser to penalties of up to $100,000 per copy distributed."

- Lock the e-book PDF file so a pirate cannot erase your name and copyright and substitute his own information.

My advice: Do not spend your time and energy worrying about people stealing your e-book.

Instead spend your time and energy on figuring out how you can sell hundreds or thousands of copies.

28

BEST PLACES TO GET SALES LEADS

I get sales leads and new clients from several sources.

But there are 6 that work better for me than all others.

Why?

Because they bring me prospects who are (a) predisposed to hire me instead of other copywriters and (b) have an immediate need for copy now instead of later.

These 6 sources are:

1. My books.

If someone read The Copywriter's Handbook or one of my other marketing books ... and they liked it ... they will be more inclined to hire me.

They already know who I am when they call me.

The fact that I am the author of a book published by a "real" (trade) publisher, and not a self-published book or Kindle e-book, impresses them.

Even better, they know my marketing approach or "philosophy" and agree with it.

In fact, they are usually eager to hire me — and price is typically not an issue.

Am I saying you should write a business book?

It could certainly help bring you more business.

But you don't have to do it.

Instead, see lead-source #2 below....

2. My articles and seminars.

Although a book is more impressive, articles and seminars similarly bring in qualified leads.

So do white papers, special reports, Webinars, e-books posters, and any other content you publish and disseminate.

Writing and speaking are perhaps the best source of leads and new business a self-employed professional can have.

My advice to you: write and publish how-to content related to your specialty to attract new clients like a magnet.

3. My e-zine.

A huge source of new business for me is my monthly e-newsletter and weekly e-mails.

They not only build credibility with content.

But my e-mails also keep my name before my prospects.

So when these readers need a copywriter, they think of me first.

4. Referrals.

Close behind books, articles, and seminars are referrals.

It's not credible or persuasive when YOU say you are great.

But it's convincing when someone else says it about you.

There are two main referral sources: (1) clients and (2) other people who have heard of me.

Both are good, but #1 is slightly better than #2, because of the first-hand experience. It's a personal endorsement.

There are whole books written about techniques for getting referrals proactively.

But I don't do any "referral marketing" where I ask people to give referrals.

I prefer referrals from people who give them spontaneously and without being asked to do so.

5. Google.

Optimize your Web site for search engines so you come up high on the Google search engine results page (SERP) when people search your keyword phrase.

Mine is "direct response copywriter."

Google is a good source of leads for the reason that these people often have an immediate need and are shopping for a copywriter to write for them NOW.

6. My web site.

Your web site must be designed to convert Google searches and other sources of traffic into sales leads.

Take a look at my site www.bly.com. Notice in the upper right corner the faux post-it note that says "Need great copy? Click here now."

It links to a contact form prospects can use to make an inquiry about my services online.

When I added this yellow box to my web site, conversion of traffic to leads doubled.

Why?

It graphically stands out.

The copy clearly identifies a need.

And it is positioned on the part of the page people look at first.

29

LET GO OF THE PAST.

In one of my favorite movies, Jersey Girl, Liv Tyler says to Ben Affleck:

"Forget about what you thought you were, and just accept who you are."

This turned out to be powerful advice to me personally, and maybe you can find some use in it yourself.

I had lots of dreams when I was young — and oddly, being a direct response copywriter was not one of them.

My ambitions in high school included being a pediatrician (I love kids) and a lawyer (I love to argue and prove a point).

In college, my ambition was to become a research chemist, so I majored in chemistry — until I realized that to rise to the top of that profession, you need a PhD ... and I didn't want more years in college.

So I switched to chemical engineering, where a B.S. was more than sufficient to get a top-notch job.

When companies came on campus to interview engineering seniors, some had technical writing positions to fill, where an engineering degree was a big plus to them.

I loved writing (I was on the college paper and magazine), so I took a technical writing job with Westinghouse ... and I was off to the races.

When I started out as a staff technical writer and then a freelance copywriter, I began writing books as an avocation.

One of my first books was a trivia book about comic book superheroes.

I hoped to be the next Stephen King or John McPhee ... but that didn't come to pass.

Today I am a working direct response copywriter who writes how-to business books on the side.

I enjoy my work, but once in a blue moon I do regret not becoming a scientist, as I still love science.

However, I don't spend a lot of time bemoaning my having missed out on a science or law career.

Do you sometimes look at your life and wish it had gone another way?

I think Liv Tyler gives good advice.

Stop regretting what might have been ... and concentrate on making the most of what is.

I have found this works for me most of the time and it can probably work for you too.

30

HOW TO WRITE GREAT
HOW-TO CONTENT

I've read that Google changes its search algorithm hundreds of times a year, as incredible as that sounds.

As of late, they've made the search engine "fussier" about the content it ranks highly.

Specifically, Google is rejecting crappy articles stuffed with keywords and written by content mills.

So how do you write content that both Google and your readers will value?

There are 4 levels of writing how-to material, and the key is to write at the higher levels.

- Level 1 is to merely write information or facts, not ideas or actionable strategies.

For instance, if you are writing a report on how to build Web sites, and you begin by telling the reader there are a billion pages on the Web, that's interesting — but it's not really that helpful.

- Level 2 is "what to do" writing. It tells the reader what to do, but not how to do it.

  An example is a real estate article that told landlords to evict problem tenants, but didn't tell how to go about it.

- Level 3 is where most good content writing should be — "how to" writing.

  You not only tell the reader what to do, but also how to do it.

  In the real estate example, the article might tell the reader the 5 points that must be included in an eviction letter.

- Level 4 is what content writers call "done for you."

  The writing not only tells the reader what and how to do something, but actually does it for them.

Again in the real estate example, the article could include a sample eviction letter that the reader can just copy and send to his tenant.

Readers and Google like solid level 3 writing, and if you can provide level 4 content, so much the better.

Google may also rank level 1 and level 2 articles high if they are accurate and well written ... but these are less valuable to your human readers.

Tip: when writing instructional material, ask yourself about every paragraph, "Am I telling the reader how to do something? Or am I just telling them what to do?" Make sure both objectives, not just the latter, are accomplished by your copy.

31

BECOME A MORE CONFIDENT SPEAKER.

When you give a speech, seminar, or class, you prepare a certain amount of material to deliver within the allotted time frame.

But it's in fact difficult to time your talk precisely.

Reason: if the group is very involved and participatory, a modest amount of material can take up the whole session.

On the other hand, if the group sits there like stones, you may find yourself completing your talk way before the end of the scheduled time.

To solve this problem, I recommend you prepare 2X the amount of lecture material you think you need.

That way, you need never worry about running out of information to talk about.

Knowing that, you'll be a more confident and less anxious speaker — because you know you can always fill your slot with worthwhile content.

One other tip: if you find it difficult to keep your lectures on track, divide the content into a numbered list; i.e. "10 tips for reducing stress in the workplace."

Then divide the time allotted by the number of tips.

For instance, if you have an hour to talk and 10 tips to deliver, each tip is 6 minutes long.

It's a lot less intimidating to deliver ten 6-minute mini-lectures than it is to speak nonstop for one hour.

Again, this will reduce your anxiety and boost your confidence.

Also, audiences have an easier time following speeches that have a well-organized structure to them.

32

THE FOUR STAGES
OF MARKETING COMPETENCE

During my quarter century as a copywriter, I have observed that business owners and managers fall into one of four categories as far as their competence and skill in marketing is concerned.

By recognizing which category you are in and taking the action steps recommended below, you can move up to the next level and significantly increase the ROI from your marketing investment.

- The lowest level of marketing competence is "unconscious incompetence." You don't know what you are doing, and worse, you don't know that you don't know.

You may think you are a pretty sharp marketer, even though to others, that is clearly not the case. Egotistical small business owners who appear in their own TV commercials and junior employees at "creative" Madison Avenue ad agencies can fall into this category.

Do you think you are an okay marketer, and blame the lack of results generated by your marketing always on external factors, such as bad timing, bad lists, or bad luck? You are probably in the unconscious incompetence stage.

Recognize that you don't know what you're doing and it is hurting your business. Get help. Hire a marketing manager who knows more than you do. Or take a marketing course or workshop.

- The next stage up the ladder is "conscious incompetence." You've recognized that the reason your marketing isn't working is that you don't know what you're doing.

Again, take the steps listed above. When I was at this stage as an advertising manager recently graduated from college and with only a year of work experience under my belt (instead of the considerable paunch that resides there now), I hired an experienced ad agency and leaned on them for guidance.

This strategy worked well for me and my employer. The company got better advertising than I could have produced on my own. And working with the agency accelerated my own marketing education, making me a more valuable employee.

"Conscious incompetence" is better than "unconscious incompetence," because people in the former stage are amenable to guidance, while those in the latter stage are not.

- Moving higher up the ladder of marketing competence, you reach the stage of "conscious competence." You've read the books, taken the courses, and understand what works. But your experience at putting it into practice is limited.

That means whenever you want to create a promotion, you have to slow down and think about what you are doing. It doesn't come naturally.

In this stage, you should keep checklists, formulas, and swipe files (examples of successful promotions you admire) close at hand. Model your own efforts after the winners of others.

Don't try to reinvent the wheel. Observe what works and adapt it to your own product and market.

- Do this enough times, and you will slowly begin to become a true master of marketing. You will reach the highest level of marketing competence, "unconscious competence."

At this stage, coming up with great offers, promotional ideas, headlines, and copy is second nature to you. You do it naturally, without having to consult your checklists or reference files. The quality of your work is better, and it comes faster and easier.

However, you should still keep an extensive swipe file of promotions. Borrowing ideas and inspiration from promotions that are working is a time-honored tradition in our industry, as long as it does not step over into plagiarism or copyright infringement.

My colleague Michael Masterson says it takes approximately 1,000 hours of practice to become really competent at copywriting, marketing, playing the flute, or anything else. If you have expert guidance, you may be able to cut that to 500 hours.

But ultimately, you learn by doing — and doing a lot. If you are at this stage, keep doing more and more marketing. When you put in 5,000 hours, you will become great, not just good, and your results will be even better.

Action step: Rank yourself using the four levels of marketing competence as described here, and follow the recommendations for whatever stage you are in.

TWENTY TWO UNDENIABLE
TRUTHS OF LIFE

1. Show up for appointments 10 minutes early.
2. Customers are not always right, but they must be treated as if they are.
3. When speaking before groups, dress up one level from what the group is wearing; e.g., if they wear shorts and tee shirts, you wear business casual.
4. Never offer unsolicited advice.
5. Leave your ego at the door.
6. Don't waste people's time by sending them jokes or stories via e-mail.
7. Do not brag by talking about your accomplishments to people who didn't ask you about them.
8. Be humble.
9. Proofread your e-mails before you send them.

10. 80% of your activity should be in your comfort zone, and 20% should be outside it. This keeps you both productive and challenged.

11. Of the people who opt into your e-list, 90% of those who eventually buy from you will do so within 90 days of subscribing to the list.

12. The more recently a customer had made a purchase, the more likely he is to do so again.

13. Old but good advice: under-promise and over-deliver.

14. Don't give your customers their money's worth. Give them more than their money's worth.

15. The easiest way to add value to an offer is with a free bonus gift.

16. The most powerful words in the English language are "free" and "you."

17. Do unto others as they would have you do unto them.

18. Spend time with your children while they are still young enough to *want* you to spend time with them.

19. Neither a borrower or a lender be.

20. Don't be so sure you are right. Perhaps you are not.

21. Life is short — over in the blink of an eye. So enjoy it now.

22. Avoid discussing religion or politics with colleagues or customers. There is little to gain from it and much to lose.

34

START SMALL

LH, a subscriber, writes:

> "I have been reading your e-mails, buying some products and building a huge how-to file for over 5 years, but haven't begun my ultimate goal of Internet marketing.:

He adds: "Fear of failure is huge and crippling, isn't it?"

Because I hear this scenario often, I think it's worth a brief commentary.

First, I don't care who you are or what your situation is, spending 5 years reading and researching about a business you want to start is way too long.

It simply means you are avoiding taking real action and staying in your comfort zone of reading and studying.

And without acting on the information you buy and study, you won't make a dime.

Secondly, fear of failure used to be a legitimate concern in the pre-Internet days.

If you were starting a small business, you would typically have to quit your job and devote yourself full-time to that business.

You'd also invest tens of thousands of dollars to buy a franchise or open a store or restaurant.

It was like the Frank Sinatra song — "All or Nothing at All." You were either in all the way or out all the way.

But the Internet has removed that cost and risk.

You can create and launch a product on the Internet for as little as a few hundred dollars, not a few thousand.

So if it doesn't work, you haven't gambled away the rent money.

Even better, you can start an Internet marketing business in your spare time, working just an hour or so each evening on it. So you can keep your day job for now — and your salary.

Action step: Stop merely reading about Internet marketing and start actually doing it. Taking the Webinars and courses and buying the DVDs and e-books is all well and good. But without action, it's just an expensive hobby, and comes to naught.

First thing to do: reserve a domain name for your new Web site at ultracheapdomains.com today. It will cost you less than ten bucks.

Reason I want you to do it: Just taking the first step will get you out of your reading rut (a rut is a grave without a cover) and into the real world of entrepreneurship, where you must go to make money.

35

THIRTY EIGHT GREAT HEADLINES
YOU CAN SWIPE

The easiest way to get ideas for headlines …

… is to keep a swipe file of successful headlines, and consult it for inspiration when you sit down to write a new promotion.

As a shortcut, here's a partial collection of such headlines from my vast swipe file, organized by category so as to make clear the approach being used:

1. Ask a question in the headline.

    "What Do Japanese Managers Have That American Managers Sometimes Lack?"

2. Tie-in to current events.

    "Stay One Step Ahead of the Stock Market Just Like Martha Stewart — But Without Her Legal Liability!"

3. Create a new terminology.

"New 'Polarized Oil' Magnetically Adheres to Wear Parts in Machine Tools, Making Them Last Up to 6 Times Longer."

4. Give news using the words "new," "introduction," or "announcing."

"Announcing a Painless Cut in Defense Spending."

5. Give the reader a command — tell him to do something.

"Try Burning This Coupon."

6. Use numbers and statistics.

"Who Ever Heard of 17,000 Blooms from a Single Plant?"

7. Promise the reader useful information.

"How to Avoid the Biggest Mistake You Can Make in Building or Buying a Home."

8. Highlight your offer.

"You Can Now Subscribe to the Best New Books — Just as You Do to a Magazine."

9. Tell a story.

"They Laughed When I Sat Down at the Piano ... But When I Started to Play."

10. Make a recommendation.

"The 5 Tech Stocks You Must Own NOW."

11. State a benefit.

"Managing UNIX Data Centers — Once Difficult, Now Easy."

12. Make a comparison.

"How to Solve Your Emissions Problems — at Half the Energy Cost of Conventional Venturi Scrubbers."

13. Use words that help the reader visualize.

"Why Some Foods 'Explode' In Your Stomach."

14. Use a testimonial.

"After Over Half a Million Miles in the Air Using AVBLEND, We've Had No Premature Camshaft Failures."

15. Offer a free special report, catalog, or booklet.

"New FREE Special Report Reveals Little-Known Strategy Millionaires Use to Keep Wealth in Their Hands — and Out of Uncle Sam's."

16. State the selling proposition directly and plainly.

"Surgical Tables Rebuilt — Free Loaners Available."

17. Arouse reader curiosity.

"The One Internet Stock You MUST Own Now. Hint: It's NOT What You Think!"

18. Promise to reveal a secret.

"Unlock Wall Street's Secret Logic."

19. Be specific.

"At 60 Miles an Hour, the Loudest Noise in This New Rolls Royce Comes from the Electric Clock."

20. Target a particular type of reader.

"We're Looking for People to Write Children's Books."

21. Add a time element.

"Instant Incorporation While U-Wait."

22. Stress cost savings, discounts, or value.

"Now You Can Get $2,177 Worth of Expensive Stock Market Newsletters for the Incredibly Low Price of Just $69!"

23. Give the reader good news.

"You're Never Too Old to Hear Better."

24. Offer an alternative to other products and services.

"No Time for Yale — Took College At Home."

25. Issue a challenge.

"Will Your Scalp Stand the Fingernail Test?"

26. Stress your guarantee.

"Develop Software Applications Up to 6 Times Faster or Your Money Back."

27. State the price.

"Link 8 PCs to Your Mainframe — Only $2,395."

28. Set up a seeming contradiction.

"Profit from 'Insider Trading' — 100% Legal!"

29. Offer an exclusive the reader can't get elsewhere.

"Earn 500+% Gains With Little-Known 'Trader's Secret Weapon.'"

30. Address the reader's concern.

    "Why Most Small Businesses Fail — and What You Can Do About It."

31. "As Crazy as It Sounds…"

    "Crazy as it Sounds, Shares of This Tiny R&D Company, Selling for $2 Today, Could be Worth as Much as $100 in the Not-Too-Distant Future."

32. Make a big promise.

    "Slice 20 Years Off Your Age!"

33. Show ROI (return on investment) for purchase of your product.

    "Hiring the Wrong Person Costs You Three Times Their Annual Salary."

34. Use a "reasons-why" headline.

    "7 Reasons Why Production Houses Nationwide Prefer Unilux Strobe Lighting When Shooting Important TV Commercials."

35. Answer important questions about your product or service.

    "7 Questions to Ask Before You Hire a Collection Agency … And One Good Answer to Each."

36. Stress the value of your premiums.

    "Yours Free — Order Now and Receive $280 in Free Gifts With Your Paid Subscription."

37. Help the reader achieve a goal.

    "Now You Can Create a Breakthrough Marketing Plan Within the Next 30 Days … for FREE!"

38. Make a contradictory statement or promise.

    "Cool Any Room in Your House Fast — Without Air Conditioning!"

36

SEVEN WAYS TO COMMAND HIGHER FEES

One of my subscribers, JA, writes:

> "Gee, Bob, as much as I try, I find that clients want to spend less than the cheaply priced writers of elance and other sources are charging.
>
> "Making the zillion dollars a decade you speak of is more a matter of finding willing clients than of my capabilities. Where are all those big-spending clients?"

Here's my answer to JA....

1. Your capabilities as a copywriter may be more important than you think.

    When I started as a freelance copywriter in the early 1980s, you could make a good living even if you were only a fair copywriter.

With so much more competition today, you have to be really good. If you aren't, invest some time and money to bring your skills up to speed.

I immodestly recommend my book *The Copywriter's Handbook*, available on www.amazon.com

2. Make yourself more valuable to your existing clients and prospects, and they will pay you more.

Ideally, offer something they cannot easily get elsewhere.

One of my colleagues who specializes in pay per click ad campaigns also manages the campaign as well as writing the copy. Few other copywriters offer this package.

A marketing consultant I know has all the business he can handle. Reason: while there are plenty of marketing consultants, he is one of the few specializing in marketing to the federal government.

3. Become a marketing guru — a recognized expert in copywriting, marketing, social media, or whatever your service is.

Some of the ways you can do this:

* Write articles.
* Write a book.
* Write a blog.
* Give talks.
* Have a content-rich Web site.
* Write and distribute an e-newsletter.
* Create and publish information products (i.e., audios, DVDs, reports).
* Send out press releases on your activities.

It basically boils down to writing and speaking on your topic, for an audience consisting of your potential clients. Writing and speaking position you as an expert in your field.

4. Write for clients for whom copy is important.

Clients who care about the copy you write for them either depend on that copy for their marketing or care about the image they portray to the public.

I once wrote sales letters and brochures for the owner (now deceased) of a large logistics company. He cared about what I did because his business was driven by marketing.

5. Write for clients who can measure the sales results of your copy.

    This means write for direct marketers and Internet marketers.

    If a client can measure the leads or sales from the promotions you write for them, and your copy increases their response rates, they will reward you handsomely.

    If a client cannot precisely measure the results from your copy, how would they know whether it's worth paying a premium for or not?

6. Market yourself as a long-copy specialist.

    Why? Simple: long copy assignments pay more than short-copy assignments.

    For instance, you can charge much more for a white paper than you can for a banner ad.

    And you can charge more to write a magalog than you can for a postcard.

    Advertise yourself as a long-copy specialist. Market your services to clients that do long-copy promotions.

    Two examples: investment newsletter publishers and dietary supplement marketers.

7. Write for clients with deep pockets.

    The clients with the deepest pockets are the Fortune 500 and companies of similar size.

    They spend thousands of dollars per project and don't even blink.

    Some industries have deeper pockets than others. Two that come to mind are financial services and healthcare, particularly pharmaceuticals.

    On the flip side, the worst-paying clients are those who find you on elance, guru.com, and other job sites.

Content mills — companies that offer article writing services to marketers for search engine optimization purposes — also pay pitiful wages to writers. Stay away.

Ad agencies and PR firms usually don't pay as well as working directly for advertisers.

Local businesses can pay decent though not top rates, but mom and pop businesses; i.e., the corner gas station or local restaurants, pay a pittance.

37

COMMAND PREMIUM PRICING FOR YOUR PRODUCTS

"I want to charge $399 for my audio cassette album," a small publisher told me.

"But Nightingale-Conant also sells several audio albums on the same topic for $79," I pointed out. "What makes yours worth five times more than theirs?"

The answer most people would give is "because mine is better."

Well, maybe it is. But "better" is a difficult proposition to sell in marketing copy.

So how can you charge a premium price to buyers to whom the greater quality of your product is not immediately obvious?

Here are 7 ways to ask for and get the price you want:

1. **Vertical niche. The more vertical your product, the higher the price you can charge.**

Your total audience will be smaller, but their need for a specific solution to their problem will help them rationalize paying your premium price.

Example: a "Selling Techniques" album priced at $399 is difficult to promote, but you might be able to get $399 for "Selling Techniques for the Automotive Aftermarket."

2. **Supply and demand. It's always easier — especially when selling your services — to hold out for more money when the demand for your service outweighs the supply.**
If you market to the point where you are generating more potential business opportunities than you can handle, you can raise your fees, because you can afford to have some of these potential buyers who balk at the higher fees walk away. (For service providers, the surest route to financial security is a full pipeline of leads.)

3. **Add value. Add value to your product or service until the buyer perceives that the price you are asking, however high, is a drop in the bucket compared to the value he is receiving.**
One way to add value is to offer a premium that is inexpensive for you to source but has a high perceived value.

Example: Ron Popeil gives away a set of steak knives free when you buy his cooker on TV.

Mike Bell at Phillips Publishing suggests you give premiums whose total value is greater than the cost of the product.

That way, even if the buyer doesn't love your product, he may keep it just to own the free gifts he received along with it.

4. **Become a guru. Make an effort to build your reputation and establish yourself as a guru — a leading expert — in your field.**
Whether it's Tom Peters, Alan Dershowitz, or Dr. Ruth, people can't get enough of gurus.

When you are a guru, people will pay a premium price for your seminars, speeches, videos, audios, books, newsletters, software, and products.

5. **Demonstrate Return on Investment (ROI). Buyers are less reluctant to pay a high price when you can show that they will get a rapid — and significant — return on their investment.**

For instance, a direct mail package selling a $149 newsletter on employee hiring says, "Hiring the wrong person costs you three times their annual salary."

The reader figures that if his average employee makes $50,000, and the newsletter can prevent even one hiring mistake, his return on investment for a subscription is 3 X $50,000 = $150,000 divided by $149, or better than 1,000 to 1 — which makes the $149 asking price an easy sell.

6. **Unique system. Despite the glut of free stock tips and financial information available on the Internet, a direct mail package from Agora Publishing successfully sold a $59 a year newsletter with this headline, "Unlock Wall Street's Hidden Logic."**

Why did it work? It offered the reader something he felt he couldn't get from all the free Web sites and e-mail newsletters he was offered: the secret to how the stock market really works — Wall Street's hidden logic.

If the customer perceives he cannot get what you offer elsewhere, he will pay a premium price for it, provided the product offers benefits he desires.

7. **Guarantee. A guarantee overcomes buyer resistance, including price resistance.**

When your product is backed by a 30-day money-back guarantee, you can offer a "no-risk trial" or "risk-free 30-day preview" rather than just say "buy my product."

In essence, you are not asking the reader to buy anything; merely to try it — to accept your offer of examining it for a month in their home or office, with no risk or obligation of any kind.

38

WRITE STRONGER LANDING PAGES

Yesterday, I met BB, an expert on building Web site traffic.

He showed me one of his projects, a Web page to which he had driven massive amounts of traffic ... yet he had not generated a single order for the product!

Why not? Because his landing page sucked!

A "landing page" is a Web page designed with the sole goal of converting traffic on the page to product sales.

When you know the rules of landing page copy and design, you can double or triple your conversion rates, orders, and sales.

Those landing page rules and sales techniques are available on my Web site www.thelandingpageguru.com

Normally, to get access to www.thelandingpageguru.com, you have to buy my landing page course on DVD for $100.

But now, for a limited time, as my valued subscriber, you can get access to www.thelandingpageguru.com for free.

When you click on the link, you will be asked for your user name — which is User — and for the password, which is pageguru.

Then just settle in to your chair with a cup of coffee and mine the wisdom and data on www.thelandingpageguru.com for all it's worth.

And it's worth at least a $100. But today, it's yours free.

39

TEN STEPS TO INTERNET
MARKETING SUCCESS

"I want to market my business on the Web, but how do I get traffic to my site?" one of my readers asked recently.

"And if I want to sell my product or service using e-mail marketing, who do I send the e-mails to?"

Here is one online marketing methodology that has been proven effective for many different types of businesses.

The primary concept is that online marketing works best when you e-mail to people who already know you.

Therefore, successful online marketers build their "house file" or "e-list" (lists of prospects and their e-mail addresses) using the process outlined below, and then sell to those people via e-mail marketing:

Step 1: Build a Web site that positions you as an expert or guru in your field (see steps 2 and 3 below). This is the "base of operations" for your online marketing campaign.

Step 2: This Web site should include a home page, an "About the Company" page, your bio, and a page with brief descriptions of your products and services (each product or service description can link to a longer sales page on the individual item).

Step 3: You should also have an "Articles Page" where you post articles you have written on your area of specialty, and where visitors can read and download these articles for free.

Step 4: Write a short special report or white paper on your area of expertise, and make this available to people who visit your site.

Visitors can download your content for free as a PDF. But in exchange, they have to register and give you their e-mail address (and any other information you want to capture).

Step 5: Consider also offering a monthly online newsletter, or "e-zine." People who visit your site can subscribe free if they register and give you their e-mail address.

You may want to give the visitor the option of checking a box that reads: "I give you permission to send me e-mails about products, services, news, and offers that may be of interest to me."

Step 6: The more "content" (useful information) on your site, the better. More people will be attracted to your site, and they will spend more time on it. They will also tell others about your site.

Step 7: The model is to drive traffic to your site where you get them to sign up for either your free report or free e-zine. Once they register, you have their e-mail address and can now market to them via e-mail as often as you like at no extra cost.

Step 8: The bulk of your online leads, sales, and profits will come from repeat e-mail marketing to this "house" e-list of prospects. Therefore your goal is to build a large e-list of qualified prospects as quickly and inexpensively as you can.

Step 9: There are a number of online marketing options that can drive traffic to your site. These include: free publicity; e-mail marketing; banner advertising; co-registrations; affiliate marketing; search engine optimization; direct mail; and e-zine advertising.

Step 10: The key to success is to try a lot of different tactics in small and inexpensive tests, throw out the ones that don't work, and do more of the ones that are effective.

Another question that comes up is frequency: How often can you send promotional e-mail offers to your house e-list?

Every time you send an e-mail to your house file, a small percentage of the list will "unsubscribe," meaning they ask to be taken off your list. The number of people who unsubscribe is called the "opt-out rate."

Start increasing the frequency of promotional e-mail to your house file. As soon as the opt-out rate spikes upward, stop. You have now reached your maximum frequency.

Many marketers have discovered that the frequency of e-mail promotion to the house file can be much higher than previously thought. Some are successfully e-mailing different offers to their house e-list as often as daily or even more.

This is good news for marketers, since the more frequently you can e-mail offers to your list, the more money you can make.

Best of all, the profit on these sales to your house file is extremely high, since the e-mail promotion costs almost nothing.

There are no postage or printing costs, and because you already own the names, you avoid the $100 to $400 per thousand charge incurred when renting outside e-lists.

40

SELLING WITH "FALSE LOGIC"

False logic, a term coined by Michael Masterson, is copy that manipulates (but does not lie about or misrepresent) facts about a product.

The objective: to help readers come to conclusions that those facts, presented without the twists of the copywriter's pen, might not otherwise support.

A catalog for Harry & David says of its pears, "Not one person in 1,000 has ever tasted them."

The statistic, as presented by the catalog writer, makes the product sound rare and exclusive — and that's how the average reader interprets it, just as the copywriter intended.

But a logician analyzing that statement might say it indicates that the pears are not very popular — almost no one buys them.

It's possible to argue that some false logic borders on deception, but the marketer has to make that call for himself.

A metals broker advertised "95% of orders shipped from stock" to indicate ready availability.

But he ran his business out of an office and had no warehouse. How could he claim he shipped from stock?

"We do ship 95% of orders from stock," the marketer explains. "But not from our stock — from the metal supplier's stock. We are just a broker. But we do not advertise that, since being a broker is perceived as a negative."

A promotion selling a stock market newsletter to consumers compares the $99 subscription price with the $2,000 the editor would charge if he were managing your money for you, based on a 2% fee and a minimum investment of $100,000.

The reader thinks he is getting Mr. Editor to give him $2,000 worth of money management services for $99, and quickly glosses over the fact that the newsletter is not precisely the same as a managed account.

A similar example is the promotion done by Don Hauptman for American Speaker, a loose-leaf service for executives on how to give good speeches.

In his promotion, he points out that this product can help you with your speeches all year long (it has periodic supplements) vs. the $5,000 it costs to have a professional speechwriter write just one speech.

But of course, American Speaker is not actually writing your speech for you.

There is an ongoing debate of whether people buy for emotional or logical reasons, but most successful marketers know that the former is more dominant as a buying motive than the latter.

It is commonly said, "People buy based on emotion, then rationalize the purchase decision with logic."

Because they have made the buying decision based on strong feelings and ingrained beliefs, they are in essence looking for justification and support for what they already want to do.

Therefore, as long as the logical argument seems credible and sensible, they will accept it. They do not probe into it as scientifically or deeply as would, say, Ralph Nader or an investigative reporter for *Consumer Reports.*

Some critics view direct marketing as a step below general marketing in respectability, ethics, and honesty. And perhaps they might reason that my advocating the use of false logic adds fuel to their argument.

But in fact, false logic is not just the purview of direct marketers; general marketers use it routinely, some with great success.

For years, McDonald's advertised "billions sold" to promote their hamburger — leading customers to the false conclusion that just because something is popular, it is necessarily good.

Publishers use similar logic when they trumpet a book as "a *New York Times* best-seller."

Is all this unethical? You can draw your own conclusion, but in my opinion, no.

A copywriter, like a lawyer, is an advocate for the client (or his employer).

Just as the lawyer uses all the arguments at his disposal to win the case, so does the copywriter use all the facts at his disposal to win the consumer over to the product.

Certainly, we should market no products that are illegal, dangerous, or immoral, though one man's Victoria's Secret catalog is another man's soft porn. But to not use all the tools at our disposal (including false logic) to persuade the buyer is either incompetence, failure to discharge fiduciary duties, or both.

41

THE AWFUL TRUTH ABOUT
AFFILIATE MARKETING

I am struggling to make this article sound kind and helpful instead of harsh and critical, but it's a touchy subject: affiliate marketing.

Listen: I get approached all the time by well-meaning newbies who want me to help them get started in Internet marketing by selling my products as an affiliate. Then they expect me to become their private tutor (for free) and teach them the Internet marketing business (for free).

Their logic is that it behooves me to do this since once they are established, they will sell lots of my products and make me a pile of money.

I hate to burst your bubble, but that virtually never happens.

All large and mid-size Internet marketers know the 99/1 rule: that 99% of your affiliate revenues will come from 1% of your affiliates.

This 1% is often referred to as "super affiliates" — experienced, already successful marketers capable of selling a lot of your product.

Almost without exception, super affiliates are other large and midsize Internet marketers with big lists and thorough knowledge of how to sell information products online.

The good thing about super affiliates is they will never ask you to teach them how to sell your products on the Internet, because they already know how.

The bad thing about super affiliates is that every other marketer wants to sell his or her products to the super affiliate's list.

Therefore the super affiliate is slammed with marketers begging to do a joint venture (JV) with them, making it very difficult for you to stand out from the crowd and make a deal with the super affiliate.

An effective strategy for forging a relationship with a super affiliate is to communicate with them on a person-to-person level, and the best way to do that is to meet them at an Internet marketing conference they sponsor, speak at, or attend.

I have also found you can stand out from the pack of wanna-be partners by following the super affiliate's writings and sending sincere e-mails of praise and appreciation when they write something that particularly speaks to you.

Another way to entice a super affiliate is with an oversize commission: offer them 70% of sales revenues instead of the usual 50%.

And the product price has to be at least $100 and preferably $300 or higher; they won't get excited about getting a cut of a $12 paperback book.

Note: Do not send your book, DVD set, or audio CD album to the super affiliate unsolicited. They are buried under mountains of material, do not want more, and will throw your product out without reviewing it.

But what about the other 99% of affiliates — the average Joe or Jane who wants to be YOUR affiliate and sell your products to their list (which they don't have yet)?

Most of them will never make a single sale, and almost all of the rest will sell at best a few dollars worth of your products — nothing significant.

But even though these 99% of affiliates will account for less than 1% of your sales, they will demand 99% of your attention with their questions, concerns, and requests.

Should you give it to them? If an affiliate needs basic instruction on running an Internet information marketing business, I recommend they listen to my Internet Marketing Retirement Plan audio program, which they can download here:

www.theinternetmarketingretirementplan.com

Some super affiliates offer coaching programs. Because I do not offer coaching to individuals, I can't work with affiliates as their advisor, and they have to go elsewhere for advice and mentoring. If I helped them all for free, I would have no time for my paying copywriting clients and my writing income would nosedive.

Another issue that comes up with the regular affiliates is asking for "review copies," which is another way of saying "Give me your product for free because I don't want to pay for it." My answer is: no.

Their reply: "Well, then I can become an affiliate and buy it for half price, right?"

Again, no: the 50% commission is for sales you make to other people, not product you buy for yourself.

This may seem harsh to you, but trust me: once you have a year or so of experience in your own Internet marketing business, you may very well come to agree with me.

Do I have a grudge against tiny affiliates? No. Most of them are nice, intelligent, well-meaning people. But they grossly overestimate their value or revenue potential to the larger potential JV partner. This I know from nearly a decade of experience as an online information marketer.

42

THANK A TEACHER TODAY

On National Thank-a-Teacher Day each year, you are supposed to thank a teacher who made a difference in your life.

I urge you to participate in this goodwill gesture for 2 reasons:

1. It will make you feel really good.
2. It may mean more to your teacher than you could ever imagine.

I also suggest you do it now. If you wait until the official date of National Thank-a-Teacher Day, you may forget.

Years ago, I dedicated my book on time management, "101 Ways to Make Every Second Count" (Career Press) to EB, my 10th grade English teacher.

Instead of mailing the book to her, I visited my old high school and waited outside her classroom door until the period was over to present it in person.

I said, "Ms. B____, I don't know if you remember me, but I was in your 10th grade English class many years ago. You taught me what good writing is. Well, I became a writer and have had dozens of books published. Here is my latest, and as you can see, it is dedicated to you. In fact, I have you to thank for my career."

I handed her the book open to the dedication which read: "To EB, who taught me how to write."

I could see she was visibly moved and she expressed her appreciation.

I got the feeling that (a) teaching can often be a thankless job (she said words to that effect) and (b) having a student express appreciation for the teaching he received was an uncommon occurrence.

I felt I had done a good thing by taking the time to thank her as I did, and to this day I am glad I did it. The occasion remains vivid in my memory.

My advice to you is: think about a teacher or mentor who helped you and made a positive difference in your life, seek her out, tell her what her counsel or wisdom meant to you, and thank her for it. You will get a lasting "high" out of doing this.

By the way, I also posted an appreciation for one of my old college professors on the University of Rochester Web site, though I don't know if he has seen it:

http://meliora.rochester.edu/alumni_page.html?encqid=be3159ad04564bfb90db9e32851ebf9c

43

DO YOU REALLY NEED TO ASK?

The question that has always vexed me most is when a subscriber writes and asks:

"Should I become a freelance copywriter?"

"Should I start an Internet marketing business?"

"Should I [fill in the blank here]?"

Now, if you ask me HOW to do these things, I can give you some solid guidance.

But if someone asked me SHOULD they do this or that, I used to throw up my hands and say — "How can I tell you that? It's entirely up to you!"

However, when I was reading the New York Review of Books (3/7/13, p. 46) last week, I came across a quote in an article by the late Isaiah Berlin that I think gives a useful answer to the question of "Should I?"

Berlin wrote: "One chooses as one chooses because (1) one knows what one wants, and (2) is ready to pay the price." (I added the numbers.)

As for the first reason, (1) choosing because "one knows what one wants," I would argue that you already know what you want or you wouldn't be asking me if you should do it.

Conversely, if you have spent years thinking about a thing and have taken no forward action, you probably don't want it that badly.

It reminds me of a story about Mozart.

Supposedly a young man in his late teens or so approached Mozart and said "Maestro! I want to write a symphony! Please, please teach me how to write a symphony!"

Mozart looked him over and said "You're too young to write a symphony."

"But Maestro Mozart, you wrote a symphony when you were twelve years old," the teen pointed out.

"Yes, but I didn't have to ask how!" Mozart replied.

If you really want to do a thing, you will pursue it and do it. If not, then not. You won't have to ask me or anyone else whether you should.

The second part of Berlin's statement says that you will choose something if you are (2) "ready to pay the price."

This price may be:

- Long years of education, practice, or apprenticeship before attaining your wish.
- Facing the possibility that, after all that time and effort and investment, you may not succeed.
- Taking a financial gamble as you invest in your new venture or dream — a gamble you could lose.
- Sacrificing time with family, leisure time, and other activities in the relentless pursuit of your vision.
- Risking the disapproval of friends and family who do not support you in your quest and say you are foolish to do it.
- Becoming so successful that you alienate those friends and family members who are less successful and resent your accomplishment.

- Taking so long to reach your goal that by the time you achieve it the other pleasures of life have passed you by and now you are too old to enjoy your success anyway.

If after reading the above list with your eyes wide open, you agree that these are prices you are willing to pay to achieve your dreams — then I encourage you to go full steam ahead.

On the other hand, if you quiver with fear after reading this list or want to put your head under the covers, you may not have the constitution required for entrepreneurial or artistic ventures or similar grand aims. And perhaps you are better off staying where and as you are.

One other point: a psychologist once told me people do not take action until the pain of their current condition — whether poverty, boredom, fear, or unhappiness — exceeds their fear of taking action and reluctance to make a change.

I think his observation is right on the money.

44

START YOUR OWN
HOME BUSINESS AFTER 50

I've started small home business in my 20s as well as in my 50s. Were there any differences in the process based on my age alone? Yes, and if you're an over-50 entrepreneur, it helps to keep them in mind.

To begin with, when I was younger, I had the boundless optimism that is bred by the naivety of youth. I hadn't been through much hardship in my life, and so didn't think anything bad could really happen to me, including the possibility of my business failing. Therefore I went boldly forward with few resources or contingencies in place.

At 50, I had, like many people, been through some very serious problems in my life, including my wife being diagnosed (mistakenly, it turned out) with terminal cancer. Therefore, I considered the pros and cons of my new business plan more carefully, and should things have turned sour, I would not have been badly hurt.

Even though I had only a few thousand dollars in my bank account when I was in my early 20s, I felt more able to take risks because I also had relatively few financial responsibilities: no family, no mortgage, and (living in Manhattan) no car payments. Plus, when you're young, if your business tanks and you lose it all, you have plenty of time to make it back.

You'd think older entrepreneurs with their greater net worth would be more financially courageous, but the opposite is often true. If you're 50, and your business bombs and draws down your retirement nest egg, you may not have time or earning power to make it back. Therefore, many 50+ entrepreneurs are afraid to take big financial risks.

Yet for many of the over-50 entrepreneurs who *are* willing to take financial risks, the money to start a business is there. If I wanted to launch a business with $100,000 start-up costs, I could do it without borrowing. Yet on the TV show Shark Tank, you see people giving away 10 to 50 percent of their entrepreneurial ventures to investors who in exchange pay them a sum in the high five or low six figures.

Younger entrepreneurs are often fueled by boundless — and some might say naïve — optimism. Optimism propels people to action, which is a good thing, but it can give them unrealistic expectations, which isn't so good.

As an old dog entrepreneur, you have to learn new tricks, and it may take a lot of practice to break old habits. For instance, my children laugh that when I need a business phone number, I look in the Yellow Pages and not Google. When my youngest son saw that AARP sent me a free transistor radio as a premium, he laughed again: "No one listens to the radio on a radio," he said.

One of the things I envy younger entrepreneurs is their seemingly infinite energy. Some of the more famous Internet marketers I know go at their online business 24/7. I work hard too, but once I hit 50, I saw that my own energy had limits.

Perhaps the biggest difference between younger and older entrepreneurs is this: in their quest to be rich, many young entrepreneurs will do any kind of business as long as they think it can make them quick and significant bucks.

When you are over 50, you are far less willing to do whatever it takes just for money. You want to do what you want to do, when you want to do it. You are reluctant to bow to the will of others just for the money. Your work has to bring you pleasure. You don't like being told what to do.

Here are the steps that I, at 55, would take if I were to start another business today:

1. Take stock of your financial situation. How much money do you have? Is it enough to retire? If your business failed and you lost money, would you still have enough to retire?

2. Write a paragraph or two describing your ideal day. Would you spend it sitting in the backyard alone with your laptop — or working shoulder to shoulder with a team? Do you want afternoons free for fishing and golf? Can you stick to a schedule or do you crave freedom and flexibility?

3. Make a lists of your interests, passions, aptitudes, and favorite activities. Are any of these things other people would pay you to do or make? Therein may lie your new business.

4. Look around to see if anyone else is already doing the business you are contemplating. If nobody is, that may be a sign that others tried and found it unfeasible. If at least one other person is making money with it, than you can too.

5. Don't spend a year studying the market and another year planning the business launch. Instead, set up and run an inexpensive marketing test campaign within the next few weeks if at all possible. The key is to see whether you can get people to buy what you want to sell. If you can, you have overcome the biggest hurdle.

6. Have realistic expectations for income. When a guru in the field talks about the fortune he is making, divide the number by two or even better, drop the last zero. That's closer to what he is most likely earning.

7. Learn the Internet. Most small businesses can be made more efficient and profitably by conducting some if not all their important activities (e.g., sales, customer service) online instead of offline. Thanks to the Web, businesses that used to require $10,000 in start-up costs can now be launched for under $1,000.

45

THE 4 KEYS TO
SUCCESS AND HAPPINESS

Ted Nicholas, Russ Dalbey, and other successful writers have in numerous publications identified — accurately, in my opinion — the 4 elements needed to attain a happy life:

1. Relationships ... you need to have family and friends — people you love and people you like.

John Donne said "No man is an island." Even introverts, loners, and recluses need people in their lives — and interaction with them.

Having friends not only makes people happy but can even improve mental health: A study from the Harvard School of Public Health found that people with the most active social lives had the slowest rate of memory decline.

I have a few good friends, but I am not very social, and I don't see them much. We communicate mainly by phone and e-mail.

My wife and I both feel that our two sons, Alex and Stephen, are the center of our life.

2. **Money … Mark Twain did NOT, as many people believe, say that money is the root of all evil. What Twain really said was: "Lack of money is the root of all evil."**

Many people erroneously believe that rich people think of nothing but money.

The fact is that those who think constantly about money are those who do not have enough of it. I've seen this up close: I have relatives who are bankrupt, and every discussion comes around to lack of money and how it hamstrings them in daily life.

Like many people, I grew up without much money. We were not poor, but many others we knew obviously had more than we did. But I never had to worry where my next meal would come from — literally, because my mother is a great cook.

3. **Work … next to my family, there is nothing as key to my happiness as loving the work I do.**

In my early life I held corporate jobs. I did not like working in a corporation, and the days passed with glacial speed.

I have been a full-time freelance copywriter since 1982, and it is still loads of fun to me every day I do it. What could be better than that? Conversely, to me there are few things worse in life than hating your job.

Thomas Carlyle: "Blessed is he who has found his work; let him ask no other blessedness."

Noel Coward: "Work is more fun than fun."

4. **Health … it is impossible to fully enjoy life if you are seriously ill or even sick a lot of the time.**

There is more health advice out there today than at any time in human history. The trick is evaluating the source and knowing what to listen to.

I have said in other e-mails that if you wake up in the morning, and you are in good health and have a roof over your head, it's a good day.

I know this from having several health scares with my wife, including the time she was misdiagnosed with stage 4 ovarian cancer and told (erroneously) that she had only months to live. Our whole world was destroyed by that one sentence until, many weeks later, we found out she was OK.

I find that enjoying the 4 conditions listed above is not a given. Most of us have to work for them, me included. Here's what I recommend:

- Family — treasure your spouse and your children. Spend lots of time with your children when they are young and still want you.
- Friends — don't let lack of time make friendships disappear. Make a proactive effort to reach out to and stay in touch with friends. In this I often fail.
- Money — make it a goal to become financially comfortable. I suggest you create a plan to amass a $2 million net worth by age 55. That is made easier by earning an annual income of $200,000 or more.
- Work — find the intersection of your passion and the needs of the marketplace. As Aristotle said, "Therein lies your vocation." In other words, find something you love that others will pay you handsomely for. As Dr. Seuss points out: "You have brains in your head. You have feet in your shoes. You can steer yourself in any direction you choose."
- Health — guys especially, don't avoid going to the doctor because you're afraid or you are being macho. When in his 60s, my father waited too long to have a lump on his leg examined. When he finally went to the doctor, it turned out to be sarcoma, and he died 18 months later after a prolonged and painful illness. During my dad's long decline, no one in our immediate family was very happy.

46

FIVE WAYS TO TAKE THE FEAR AND ANXIETY OUT OF PUBLIC SPEAKING

Does the thought of speaking in front of a group make you squirm?

If so, you're not alone: According to levelupliving.com, 75% of the population has a fear of public speaking.

Yet speaking in front of a group can advance your career and build your reputation as an expert in your field. So what can you do?

Here are a few tips to alleviate the fear and make you a more confident presenter:

1. Prepare twice as much material as you need.

Some audiences participate actively, and the back-and-forth takes time. Therefore, in such cases, filling the time is no problem.

On the other hand, a nonresponsive audience means you'll go through your lecture more quickly, and as a result, risk running out of material before the allotted time is up.

The solution? Prepare twice as much material as you think you'll need. That way, the fear of being left with lots of time and nothing to say is eliminated.

Nicholson Baker writes in a blog post for the New York Review of Books:

"The worst dreams I have these days are ones in which I have to go on stage and give a talk in front of an audience of smart attentive people, and I'm unprepared.

"I'm supposed to be full of wisdom on some specialized topic — say Voltaire's voluminous correspondence with Stanislaw Lem — and my brain races to remember what I have to say on this subject, which is nothing."

2. Prepare exercises for the audience.

Have activities that help audience members build and practice the skill you are teaching — quizzes, fill-in-the-blank worksheets, group exercises.

As an added benefit, these exercises shift the burden of action from you to your students, giving you a mini rest break during an otherwise intensive seminar.

Of course, you should already have a teacher's version of the exercise with the answers on it. That way you can relax while they're working.

3. Show a video.

In the movie "Bad Teacher," Cameron Diaz avoids doing any real teaching by continually showing movies to her high school English class.

You shouldn't be a bad teacher, but in a one or two-day class, I often like to show one or two educational videos, which typically run 15 to 20 minutes each.

The videos can help teach parts of the main topic that you may not be particularly strong on.

In addition, they allow you to step out of the room for 5 or 10 minutes, take a break, and mentally regroup before you continue your lesson.

4. Bring in a guest expert.

Once I was flattered to be asked to speak at a direct marketing class being taught by MH, one of my colleagues — until I realized that one reason for my being there was for MH to do less work!

Having a guest expert treats your audience to a fresh point of view. But it also offloads speaking duties from you to your guest experts.

MH taught a 10-week course and had 3 different guest experts each teach one session. Therefore he reduced his teaching load by 30%.

5. Beware of small classes.

The smaller the number of attendees, the less interaction there is between the students. If you get a small group that lacks participation, you can burn through your prepared materials quickly.

I like to have a minimum of 15 students in any training classes and at least 25 attendees at lunch or evening speeches. Fewer dampen the energy in the room.

For more public speaking tips, read my book "Persuasive Presentations for Business," published by Entrepreneur Press.

47

NEW GOOGLE ALGORITHM DEMANDS BETTER ARTICLE WRITING

The Google algorithm used to reward online marketers for posting lots of short, poorly written articles on their Web site; "content mills" sprang up to meet the demand.

How bad are those content mill writers working for as little as $15 per article? I once made the mistake of hiring one to write an article on careers in chemistry for one of my Web sites.

I will never forget the laugh her first sentence gave me: "Chemistry is a good career for people who are fond of atoms." She also wrote, "To have a career in chemistry, one should study chemistry in college."

But things have changed. Lately Copyblogger.com and Marketingprofs. com have been writing about how Google now penalizes marketers for these sorry articles and rewards them for quality content with higher search engine rankings.

That's good news for good content writers, whose ability to write original and engaging content will now be more valued by the marketplace.

And it's good news for online marketers that provide their visitors with value instead of junk in their articles.

How much quality content should you post on your Web site? The more good articles you have, the better.

The problem for Internet marketers is that creating a large volume of quality articles is a lot of work and takes a lot of time.

When I first put up my Web site, I had no articles, and I dreaded the labor ahead of me in coming up with articles.

Then I realized that I had written dozens of articles on marketing in the 1980s for Business Marketing, Direct Marketing, and other marketing publications — and these had never been posted on the Web anywhere!

I immediately wondered whether I still had hard copies of the articles. I didn't have electronic copies since I had changed from a CPM to an MS-DOS computer years ago.

I went downstairs to my basement archives. The originals of all the articles were in a bottom drawer in a file cabinet. But to my dismay, I found that Humphrey, our old cat who had a kidney problem, had peed all over the drawer. And the articles were covered with a foul-smelling yellow powder.

I put on dishwashing gloves, picked the articles out of the drawer with a tweezers, photocopied them, scanned the clean copies into Word, and posted the Word files on my Web site, where they now reside for your reading pleasure; of course there is no charge to read or download them:

http://www.bly.com/newsite/Pages/articles.php

Most visitors to my site who read these articles do not know they were once drenched in feline urine!

If you are just starting out and don't have a library of cat-pee-covered articles already written, how do you ramp up the content on your Web site?

My suggestion is that you find a venue where you are required to produce articles on a regular basis.

Be sure to retain the rights to your articles so you can post them on your Web site without restriction. Type "First rights only" in the upper left corner of the first page of every article you submit.

Here are a few options for creating an article-generating machine:

1. Write a blog and post an article a week on it — at least 300 words.

2. Write a column for a trade magazine or newsletter. I write a regular column on B2B marketing for Target Marketing magazine, and post the articles on my site once Target has published them. My column runs 1,000 words.

3. Write a weekly article for distribution to subscribers to your e-list — like this one. Then post those messages in an article archive on your site. Length typically ranges from 400 to 750 words.

Suggestions #1 — 3 above will force you to create content on a regular basis, with no slacking in your production. It will become a habit and in one year, you'll have anywhere from a dozen to as many as 50 articles to post on your site.

On the other hand, I find that if you don't have an outlet that requires regular articles from you, you will never get around to writing any or posting them on your site — and your Google ranking will suffer as a result.

Don't merely rewrite other people's articles and post them on your site. Make your content original, based on your own marketing campaigns and tests.

48

SERVICE BUSINESSES: 7 WAYS
TO BEAT YOUR COMPETITORS

Subscriber MK writes:

"Writing has always been my true passion. I am strongly considering copywriting, and yet I have no experience.

"Bob, from the time you penned your Copywriter's Handbook, copywriting has grown rapidly by leaps and bounds; there is a plethora of copywriters out there. Is there any room for me?"

MK's question is one I am frequently asked and deserves a thoughtful answer, so here's what I think....

To begin with, there is a plethora of new copywriters out there today, and 97% of them are novices like MK.

Therefore, he's got a lot of competition from which, at least on the surface, he has not differentiated himself.

So, can he make it?

There are 7 tactics that can compel potential clients in copywriting or any other service business to choose you instead of your competitors:

1. Charge less.

    There are many clients who are looking to get the lowest price they can. So if you charge less than your competitors, these clients will be more inclined to hire you.

    For a service business, this strategy dooms you to misery. You risk getting in a price war with your competitors. And you end up working for peanuts.

2. Deliver faster.

    One copywriter used to advertise in Adweek magazine that he offered 24-hour turnaround for ad copy. His ad attracted clients with rush jobs that other copywriters were too busy to handle. FedEx build an empire on "when it absolutely, positively has to be there overnight."

3. Provide better quality.

    Get really good at what you do so you can deliver a superior quality product or service to your customers.

    If you write copy that generates measurable results, clients can know with certainty whether your copy works or not. If it does, they will be pleased. But you can't always guarantee a winner. All the old pros know this fact.

4. Offer convenience.

    Consumers are impatient and demanding today. The easier you are to do business with, the more business you will get. Unlike some copywriters, who only accept their retainer as a check, I also take PayPal, bank wire, MasterCard, Visa, and American Express.

    Why do people pay double for a box of Cheerios at 7-11 instead of going to the supermarket? Simply because it saves them time, and that's something consumers value almost more than anything else.

5. Specialize.

Say a homeowner wants a deck built. He looks in the Yellow Pages and sees three ads for carpenters. Two say "carpenters." One says "Decks." Which do you think he is more likely to call first?

As a copywriter, you can specialize by task (e.g., writing Web pages, e-mails, white papers), industry (health care, financial), or audience (e.g., writing for business opportunity seekers, mothers, attorneys).

6. Brand yourself.

Become known for something. Example: There are a lot of Internet marketing gurus. But Perry Marshall made himself stand out from the crowd by becoming known as the specialist in Google AdWords. In the same way, copywriter Gordon Graham achieved success by establishing himself as "the white paper guy."

7. Gain a strategic advantage.

Acquire some experience, expertise, knowledge, or credential that your competitors cannot readily duplicate.

For example, when I started freelancing in 1982, I worked with mostly industrial clients. My advantage was that I had a technical background (a degree in engineering) and back then the few other freelance copywriters I competed with did not.

Don't underestimate the advantage you can get from working harder and longer than your competitors. And keep at it: When people do not succeed in a business, it is frequently because they give up too early.

Calvin Coolidge: "Nothing in the world can take the place of Persistence. Talent will not; nothing is more common than unsuccessful men with talent. Genius will not; unrewarded genius is almost a proverb. Education will not; the world is full of educated derelicts. Persistence and determination alone are omnipotent."

49

IS YOUR MUSIC STILL INSIDE YOU?

A couple of weeks ago, in a quiet old cemetery next to a horse farm, TS, my father-in-law, was buried.

I think TS felt unaccomplished in that he never achieved his most fervent dream: having a play of his produced in New York.

Oliver Wendell Holmes once said: "Most people die with their music still in them."

But I give TS more credit than he gave himself.

TS took 2 years off from work to write his play, move from Maine to New York City, and attempt to get it produced.

True, the play never ran, but it was not for lack of trying.

In this, TS was ahead of the curve: at least he sat down, wrote, and completed his play.

I know many people who want to write a play or a novel, or launch a business or create a product, and never get the thing finished — or worse, even started.

That includes me.

I have always dreamed of being a published novelist, but have never had a novel published.

That's due in large part to my never having written a novel.

I made a few false starts, but never got past the first ten pages on any of them.

My excuse I tell people is that I never had an idea for a story I thought could sustain a novel-length work.

The other excuse is that I already write all the time, so that I have no time for fiction.

I can't give you a formula that guarantees you will be successful as a playwright, novelist, inventor, entrepreneur, or anything else.

But I can give you a formula that guarantees your failure: don't write the play or novel, or start the business, or build the invention.

I am ashamed to say that this is the formula I followed in my career as a novelist, with the results indicated above.

I close with this advice from Johann Wolfgang von Goethe:

"Whatever you do, or dream you can, begin it. Boldness has genius and power and magic in it."

Do as I say. Not as I do.

50

MARKETING WITH PREMIUMS

When my kids were little, they would crack themselves up by preparing strange concoctions in the kitchen, feeding them to me, and watching me grimace.

My eyes were closed, so luckily, I never knew what I was about to ingest.

One time, when it was dog biscuits, I was shocked at how terrible they tasted, despite pictures and copy on the box that made them sound like a gourmet meal at a 5-star restaurant.

I pondered that dogs were willing to do a lot — come, sit, fetch, roll over, play dead — for really small rewards.

And then it gradually dawned on me that people are the same way — a fact you can use to good advantage in your marketing.

Example: back in the 80s, a friend of mine worked at a medical ad agency.

The agency specialized in creating direct mail (DM) that invited doctors to medical symposia. These seminars were supposed to deliver content on the treatment of a specific disease, but the bottom-line goal was to promote the sponsor's drug.

My friend did an A/B split test with a DM invitation to a symposium. The only difference between the test cells was that A offered a free pocket diary as a bonus gift to doctors who attended and B did not offer the premium.

When the agency mailed the test, mailing A offering the free pocket diary generated 6 times more response than mailing B without it. We were all amazed because it was a cheap little pocket diary that cost the client about a dollar each, and the audience was doctors earning six-figure incomes.

"Don't be amazed," the client told us. "When doctors at our symposia ask our staff where the pay phone is, nine times out of ten they also ask us if we have a quarter they can use to make a call!" (Remember pay phones?)

In my first job out of college, I worked in the marketing department for Westinghouse Defense, whose major client was the U.S. military. We were tasked with maintaining a supply cabinet full of promotional items for Westinghouse salespeople to give to the high-ranking military personnel who were our prospects.

The most in-demand item was Westinghouse golf tees — plain white tees imprinted with the famous "circle W" Westinghouse logo in blue. The salespeople and their customers were so crazy for free golf tees we could not keep them in stock.

People, even wealthy ones, are eager to get free stuff and discounts. Recently a new bank opened in the upper-class town next to ours. They did the usual free balloons and hot dogs for the grand opening, and their parking lot was packed to overflowing. I love hot dogs, but I'm not going to fight for a parking space to get a free one.

Any free gift given with inquiry or order is called a "premium." A "freemium" is a free gift enclosed with the mailing; e.g., rosary beads or a crucifix enclosed with a Catholic charities fundraising letter.

A "keeper" is a premium the consumer keeps even if he returns the product for a refund; e.g. The Folio Society offers a free 2-volume book set

The Greek Myths when you order the Shorter Oxford English Dictionary for $19.95.

They ship the whole thing when you mail the return coupon from their ad; no payment with order is required. If you wish, you can just pack up and return the Dictionary when it arrives, pulling out and keeping *The Greek Myths* as a totally free gift.

I know: I've done it. A consumer who orders just to get the keeper premium and then returns the product is known as a "premium bandit." Some direct marketers identify premium bandits with a code attached to the record in their database, and do not fulfill the premium bandit's requests for keeper premiums.

Premium bandits are not actually thieves because all we are doing is taking advantage of an offer the marketer willingly makes.

The marketer knows in advance that a small percentage of orders will be from premium bandits, and this is part of their cost of doing business. "No biggie," as the kids say.

I can also tell you that on more than one occasion, I was planning just on keeping the keeper premium, but when I saw the product, I liked it so much that I changed my mind and paid the invoice.

The premiums that work best (a) have a high perceived value, (b) are unique, and (c) are relevant to the product. We also look for a low cost per unit.

A great example is Gevalia Coffee giving away a beautiful high-quality coffee maker (I know; we have two) when you signed up for monthly shipments of gourmet flavored coffee. We ordered to get the coffee maker, but the flavors were so good we kept our subscription for a few months, which is what Gevalia was banking on.

Action step: think about what items would make good premiums complementing your offers. Source these items, incorporate them into your offer copy, and measure the change in response rate vs. the same offer with no premium.

For more information on how to select and use premiums in your marketing, read my hardcover book "How to Create Irresistible Offers" (AWAI).

51

WORK IS ITS OWN REWARD

A week or so ago MW, a subscriber, wrote:

> "Obviously you enjoy writing and marketing and you have established yourself as an expert in many fields. You are making a ton of money. So what's it all for?"

He continued: "You don't travel. You don't seem to socialize outside of your work. Are you happy? Do you have no stress to get rid of? Are you healthy? The only area you didn't mention is family, so I am assuming you work as hard as you do for them, and they bring you the joy and happiness you covet and desire in your life."

Let me address the points in MW's query....

- To begin with, I make a nice living, but I certainly don't make "a ton of money."

- The only areas where I might be considered an expert are copywriting and marketing. Maybe freelancing. But nothing else.
- At age 55, I'm basically in good health, except for having to take medications to control my blood pressure.
- I'm an introvert and a loner, but I am not a recluse; thanks to constant prodding by my wife, I socialize to an acceptable level.
- Yes, my family is the thing most important to me, and my kids are my pride and joy.
- As for travel: I simply do not like to travel, especially since air travel has become such a hassle today; I like to be home.

MW's big fallacy, however, is his not recognizing that for people who love what they do, work can be its own reward.

Yes, I want and need money and the many things money buys: college tuition for my kids, financial security for my family, and a comfortable lifestyle.

But we live pretty simply: I do not live in a mansion or drive a luxury car. My most expensive indulgence is an annual subscription to The New York Review of Books.

What I get most out of serving my clients as well as I can is the privilege of writing even more for them.

You see, writing is what I like to do most (reading is second), and copywriting is my favorite type of writing — although writing essays like this one is a close second.

MW asks, "What's it — working as hard as you do — all for?" It seems as if he doesn't see that there can be great pleasure in doing one's job well, assuming you love what you do.

If you don't love your job, then work can be the opposite: a purgatory, as it was for my late father, who was in the insurance business for 4 decades and hated it. Dad said he would have liked to be either a teacher or a forest ranger; he loved kids and nature.

Since he didn't like work, he found his pleasure in his family and his hobbies. Dad collected stamps and coins, played tennis, bowled, played poker, and above all, loved fishing. I don't care about fishing, but as a boy pretended I liked it, because I loved him.

As for me, I agree with Noel Coward, who said "Work is more fun than fun!" I am sad my father never experienced that joy at the office.

I have mentioned in these e-mails that if I go a day without writing, I start to feel off-kilter. The week we were without power after hurricane Sandy nearly drove me over the edge.

I also feel a strong bond with my writing hero the late Isaac Asimov who said, "Oh, there are plenty of things I like to do. But when it comes to things I love to do — writing is it."

52

WHAT I LOVE ABOUT COPYWRITING

My subscriber MD writes:

> "That was an excellent essay on having fun working. I'm just wondering what it is exactly that you love about your work the most? Is it the results your copywriting achieves? Is it when you complete what you feel is your best work? Or is it a combination of these things?"

MD got me thinking, and here's what I came up with as an answer:

1. What I like most is the process itself ... the act of writing ... the thinking and the clicking on the keys to form the sentences, paragraphs, and pages.
2. Of course I love it when my copy generates results, which — since I am a direct response copywriter — usually means generating a

lead or an order. There's no better feeling than to watch the sales coming in one after the other.

3. It's important to me to produce copy that, while getting the results, also communicates the ideas the client wanted to say in the way they wanted to say it. When a client says they like the copy, even before it runs, I like that.

4. I like holding the finished product in my hand. For my career as a nonfiction author, that means getting that box from the publisher with my dozen author's copies of the printed book inside. For copywriting, it may mean receiving the distributed e-mail or logging onto the new Web site I wrote for that client.

5. Most of my business these days comes from either referral (someone gave someone else my name) or reputation (the prospect calls because they have heard of me — maybe they heard me speak or read one of my books, articles, or essays). That's a very satisfying way of doing business — much more pleasant, I imagine, than making cold calls (which I personally never did), banging on doors for business (yuck).

6. Though I do not think of myself as having a big ego, I must admit I do enjoy getting fan mail from people who have read something I have written, whether it's in response to an essay, a book, or an ad.

7. The other thing I love about work is the conditions under which I work: alone in my home office, surrounded by my books and files, high up on the third floor overlooking our heavily wooded backyard out a large window which I face as I work. No boss, no commute, no suit and tie, no meetings. Heaven!

Action step: Divide a sheet of paper vertically into two columns. Label the left pros and the right cons.

In the pros column, list all the things you like about your job, as I have done above. In the con column, write down what you dislike about your job. If the con column is much bigger than the pros column, it may be time for a career change.

53

HOW TO GET REALLY GOOD AT WRITING OR ANYTHING ELSE

There's an old joke that a musician slated to perform asks a police officer how to get to Carnegie Hall.

"Practice, my boy, practice," the officer replies. Of course, he meant that in music, practice makes perfect.

Ted Nicholas, the superstar marketer, says that practice is the way to master copywriting as well.

"In my opinion, it takes at least 1,000 hours in study and practice to become an excellent copywriter," says Ted.

"However, that applies only to the rare person who is fortunate enough to be born with extraordinary talents for copywriting. Otherwise, a typical average person needs many more hours of study and practice to be competent.

"Probably with 10,000 hours of dedicated study, as Malcolm Gladwell also asserts, one can become an excellent, high-earning copywriter."

Ted is referring to author Malcolm Gladwell who in his book *Outliers* quotes neurologist Daniel Levitin as saying that you have to do an activity for a combined 10,000 hours to become a true master at it.

One problem with the copywriting business today is that a flood of new copywriters have entered the profession after taking training but without having put in the requisite 1,000 to 10,000 hours of practice Ted Nicholas recommends.

How long does it take to get good? It depends on how much you write, but let's say you work at freelance copywriting and get in 20 hours of writing (as opposed to client contact, office paperwork, and other nonwriting tasks) a week.

Given 50 weeks a year, you can get in your 1,000 hours in a year — more learning than required in some professions, less than required in others. To rack up 10,000 hours of copywriting at this rate would take a full decade.

Now here's the bottom line: whether it's copywriting or Spanish, quilting or karate, there's a course out there that can teach it to you.

However, any course is limited to teaching you the methods and techniques only. It can't automatically confer mastery on you. Only you can do that with the thousands of hours of practice advocated by Nicholas and Gladwell.

Some people are willing to put in the time and others not. That's one reason why some students get really good while others languish: a lot of people like the idea of being a writer but don't want to put in the hard work to achieve proficiency.

As the author of 80 books, I agree with writer May Sarton, who said: "Many people want to have written a book; but not many actually want to write one." Writing strikes many as glamorous, but it's mainly hard, sweaty work.

54

KEEP YOUR PC UP AND RUNNING — ALL THE TIME

Many white-collar professionals, including me, are wholly dependent on having an operating PC to get their work done.

In the past, if I had a PC crash, it would be a disaster: I couldn't get my work done and would be in danger of missing deadlines.

Now I've solved that problem, and I want to share with you how I did it, in case having a working PC is as important to you as it is to me.

I now have two PCs sitting on a table side by side: the Dell is the primary, and the HP is the back up.

They are both connected to a Trulink 2-port VGA KVM switch, which is also connected to my keyboard, mouse, and monitor shared by the two PCs.

If the Dell goes down, I just press a button on top of the Trulink. It instantly switches me to the HP, and I continue working without more than a second's interruption.

And, to enable me to always access my files, they are not stored on either computer's hard drive.

Instead, my data is stored on an external network storage device — a Synology DiskStation — which both PCs can access.

If the Synology DiskStation was ever corrupted, all my files are also automatically replicated and stored on a remote back-up system using iDrive.

So even if my desktop computer systems were destroyed by fire or hurricane, my data would be safe.

Many of my subscribers tell me they also back up their files in case of a hard disk crash.

But few have a whole redundant PC like I do with push-button switching between the primary and the secondary.

It's something I think you should look into if you depend on a working PC with access to your important work files.

My subscriber LM recommends getting an AlphaSmart Neo, a word processor that can run on ordinary AA batteries for at least 700 hours:

www.neo-direct.com

Writes LM: "There's no slot for a memory card or any detachable storage device. But the Neo holds hundreds of pages of text internally. Also, they're cheap on eBay, so you could buy extra Neos. I own three.

"The latest model Neo can upload wirelessly to Google Docs using a separate receiver that plugs into your computer. I hook mine up to my computer with a USB cable. It transfers text to and from the computer using Neo software. You can load or unload all of your text in just a few seconds.

"One caveat: the Neo remembers text as keystrokes only, so there's no formatting, not even underlining. That's the major drawback. But the unit itself is incredibly simple and durable. I've backpacked with mine and been able to write on mountaintops, trails, etc. And during power outages."

55

COMMON GRAMMAR
MISTAKES TO AVOID

An old commercial for Winston cigarettes asked viewers: "What do you want — good grammar or good taste?"

And many marketers and writers I know have differing opinions on the importance of good grammar.

My copywriting professor, Milt Pierce, taught us that "it is more important for copy to sound natural and conversational than it is to have perfect grammar."

On the other hand, for many readers, your credibility suffers when you make grammatical or spelling errors.

What are the most common grammar mistakes?

* Noun and pronoun disagreement is certainly near the top of the list.

I often see this sentence or a variation of it:

"Each supervisor must complete their performance reviews by Friday."

It sounds right.

But "supervisor" is singular, so it takes a singular pronoun:

"Each supervisor must complete his or her performance reviews by Friday."

Noun and pronoun also agree when you make "supervisor" plural:

"Supervisors must complete their performance reviews by Friday."

- Another common error is the dangling modifier. For example: "After finding the missing report, the search was ended by the secretary."

This sentence makes it sound like the "search" did the finding. Of course, it was the secretary who found the report.

So it's more correct to say: "After finding the missing report, the secretary ended the search."

- Then there are the problematic pronouns "me" and "I."

This sentence sounds right: "John, George, and me went to the ball game."

But take away John and George and you get the ungrammatical: "Me went to the ball game."

The correct way to write it is: "John, George, and I went to the ball game."

- Displaced modifiers are also a problem.

This sentence too sounds right:

"The payroll teller recommended First Carrier over Federated, whose delivery service is very prompt."

If First Carrier is recommended, it must be the prompt company, not Federated.

So we write:

"The payroll teller recommended First Carrier, whose delivery is very prompt, over Federated."

- Then there's subject and verb disagreement.

"An order form, as well as a postage-paid envelope, are enclosed."
Once again, it sounds right.
But the subject of the sentence is singular ("order form"), so the verb must be singular to match:
"An order form, as well as a postage-paid envelope, is enclosed."
Now to be fair, I am not much of a stickler on grammar.
But some of your readers undoubtedly are. And if you make errors, they'll call you out on it.
(I know this from my own experience publishing these e-mails.)
Grammatical errors can cause the reader to focus on the mistake instead of your message.
So it behooves you to use good grammar and spelling — to avoid distracting the reader from your copy.

56

WHO BUYS INFORMATION PRODUCTS?

Recently my wife went to a seminar on making money in real estate.

During the presentation, the speaker said there were 3 types of people who go to "make money" seminars.

And I think these 3 categories apply equally to other information products: e-books, books, audio, video, and Webinars.

They are:

1. Information junkies.

These are customers who buy e-book after e-book, and attend every Webinar out there, but never actually do anything with the information.

As an information marketer, I have mixed feelings about the info junkies.

On the one hand, they buy a lot of my e-books, DVDs, and CDs, putting money into my pocket.

On the other hand, while they send testimonials on how much they like my info products, they never send testimonials telling the results they achieved by applying my information — because they haven't done anything.

There's nothing wrong with reading how-to-make-money and business success books.

Some people view it as an enjoyable hobby; they just like reading about it — and dreaming of doing it "some day."

No harm in that. It's safer than snowboarding ... and less fattening than gourmet cooking.

But without action, the information does nothing for these readers — and they will never improve their lives because of it.

2. Doubters.

These are the people who are highly skeptical of claims made in money-making info products and the advertisements promoting them.

A healthy degree of skepticism is a smart position to take.

Why?

Because many marketers do, in fact, make exaggerated claims.

My rule of thumb: If it sounds too good to be true, it probably is.

If you are too skeptical, however, you will invariably reject products and programs that may be of genuine benefit to you.

It helps to (a) know the reputation of the seller and (b) make sure there is an unconditional money-back guarantee of satisfaction.

That way you can review the product with no commitment, and make your own decision as to whether it and the author are on the level.

3. Doers.

These are info product buyers who actually do what the programs say to do.

Since ideas without action are nothing, by taking action the doers go from just reading about an opportunity to actually doing it.

As a result, they are the only info products buyers who actually make money and enjoy success with their info product purchases.

If they buy a product on making money in real estate, they buy an investment property.

If they buy a product on the care and feeding of tropical fish, they enjoy a sparkling, beautiful tank of healthy fish.

And the more successful they become by following your advice, the more they will buy from you.

Info junkies ... doubters ... doers.

Which are you?

57

THE POWER OF PERSISTENCE

My dad died 16 years ago.

He was a great father … and we were extremely close.

I admired how Dad, growing up in the Great Depression, lifted himself up from poverty to a comfortable middle class existence.

I knew we didn't have as much money as a lot of families.

But we always had clothes, shelter, and never missed a meal.

To achieve this comfortable existence, my father made the ultimate sacrifice:

He worked for more than 40 years at a job he did not like (as an insurance agent).

Dad found his happiness in his family, his friends, and his hobbies (he played poker, bowled, and collected coins).

I met many more people who did not like their jobs when I worked as a technical writer for Westinghouse in the late 70s.

These people performed mindless repetitive tasks — like wrapping wire around a cylinder — 8 hours a day, 5 days a week.

When the five o'clock whistle blew, they dropped what they were doing and raced out of there with amazing speed.

Based on observations of my father and Westinghouse, I soon concluded that — above all else — I wanted to avoid working at a job that I didn't like … especially one that was boring.

So after a few years as a wage slave in corporate America, I quit to strike out on my own as a freelance copywriter, seminar leader, and book author … and much later, as an Internet information marketer.

You could say I am lucky in that I love my work.

But you and I don't get jobs we love through luck, for the most part.

You gain the ability to love your work by making a deliberate choice to pursue a career or business that interests you — and staying at it until you succeed.

So why do so many small businesses fail?

There are a lot of reasons, but a primary one is: they give up too early.

Something bad happens. A customer doesn't pay a large bill. The economy turns sour.

So they give up. Way too easily.

One of the secrets to success is persistence: pressing on in the face of adversity.

Remember the fight between Rocky and Apollo Creed in Rocky II?

Rocky won the heavyweight championship of the world because he got up after being knocked down … and Apollo didn't.

The musical group Chumbawamba says in their song Tub Thumping: "I get knocked down. But I get up again. You're never going to keep me down."

Calvin Coolidge: "Nothing in the world can take the place of Persistence. Talent will not; nothing is more common than unsuccessful men with talent.

"Genius will not; unrewarded genius is almost a proverb. Education will not; the world is full of educated derelicts. Persistence and determination alone are omnipotent."

Winston Churchill: "Never give up."

58

THE HIDDEN DANGERS
OF A 9 TO 5 JOB

What's scarier than starting your own business?

In my opinion, it's having a 9-to-5 job!

What makes me say so?

Well, there has been a huge "paradigm shift" (forgive the jargon) in employment that has turned the work world upside down.

When I was a young lad fresh out of college in the late 70s, getting a corporate job — like I did — was the safe, secure thing to do.

(Many of the older men and women in my company had been in the same job for decades.)

Entrepreneurs, by comparison, were seen as crazy risk-takers ... gambling their futures on uncertain ventures.

Today, it's quite the opposite.

By starting their own companies, entrepreneurs take control of their work life. They protect themselves from pink slips by being business owners, because they are their own bosses.

Meanwhile, the 9 to 5 world has become a shaky and uncertain place. The old "guaranteed" job security of the 1970s is gone.

KF, the daughter of a friend of my wife, recently graduated college with a BA in business administration.

To get a job, KF sent out 400 resumes. She received only a handful of calls.

Out of this, she got one interview and one job offer — for the staggering sum of $11 an hour.

It is commonplace today for headhunters and recruiters not to respond at all when you send them your resume.

Rude, but a fact of life.

So what can you do?

- If you are young and just beginning in your career, consider starting a small business either on a full or part-time basis.

  The entrepreneurial experience will serve you well in later life. And you are at an age when — unburdened by family and mortgage — you can afford to take risks.

- If you are a 9 to 5 worker who has a job, look around for a home business you can do on a moonlighting basis.

  Do not advertise to your coworkers that you have started a spare-time business. Word could get back to your supervisor, who may think you are shirking your responsibilities to work on your business.

- Are you a 9 to 5 worker who was recently downsized? Instead of looking for another corporate job, why not apply your skills as a freelancer, consultant, or merchant?

  Offering your major skill to the marketplace is a common route to self-employment: a programmer is fired, and instead of looking for another programming job, begins to offer programming services to clients at an hourly rate several times greater than he earned in his salaried position.

- In your 50s or 60s, you are easing towards retirement or perhaps already retired.

  Most Americans who approach retirement have not saved up nearly enough money to live comfortably in their golden years.

  Starting a spare-time business can provide the extra income you need to fill you financial coffers and achieve your retirement investing goal.

- In your 70s, 80s, and beyond, you are retired, which for most people means they no longer have a source of income. Therefore, they may be forced to live more frugally than they'd like.

  Operating your own small business can put thousands of dollars of extra cash in your pocket to supplement your pension and social security.

  There are very few of us in today's economy who can't use more money. Launching your own small business is one of the surest ways to earn the extra income you need.

59

THREE REASONS WHY PEOPLE DON'T WRITE WELL

In The Writer magazine (6/12, p. 15), my favorite novelist, Pat Conroy (*The Prince of Tides, The Great Santini, South of Broad*) writes that, "Good writing is the hardest form of thinking."

He continues: "It involves the agony of turning profoundly difficult thoughts into lucid form, then forcing them into the tight-fitting uniform of language, making them visible and clear. If the writing is good, then the result seems effortless and inevitable."

This sounds nice, but do you buy his claim that good writing is really the hardest form of thinking? I think for most people, the hardest form of thinking is mathematics.

My youngest son is a freshman at Carnegie-Mellon majoring in computer engineering. He took a course in "calculus in three dimensions" and another in matrix theory.

I would wager that calculus in three dimensions is more difficult for most students than English composition. And I think the computer engineering curriculum is more difficult than being an English major.

Of course, this is prejudice fueled by techie snobbism on my part.

Decades ago I was a chemical engineering major at the University of Rochester.

We engineers all thought we were smarter — and that our course of studies was harder — than liberal arts.

Recently, while looking at texts my oldest son is reading as part of his history major, I revised my thinking somewhat.

He was studying original historical documents from the revolutionary war, and it was all I could do to keep my head from exploding. Difficult stuff!

I wouldn't argue with Conroy, however, about writing being a hard form of thinking.

Even in today's keyboard era, lots of people have trouble with writing.

And in my experience, the most common causes of poor writing are as follows:

1. The writing communicates no clear idea or theme.

Michael Masterson has said that good writing is a great idea clearly expressed.

Some people can clearly express themselves in writing.

But their writing suffers because it either doesn't contain an interesting, important idea ... or because the idea hasn't been well thought out.

Kurt Vonnegut's rule of thumb: if you can't explain your idea to a 12-year-old in a few sentences, you don't really understand it yourself.

And if you don't have a clear picture of what you want to say, how will you communicate your ideas to others?

2. The writer doesn't know enough about his subject.

Many writers fail to do the research necessary to write compelling, content-rich copy — whether for an e-mail or a magazine article.

Research once meant hunting through dusty library stacks in a desperate search for data that often just couldn't be found.

Now Google makes research much faster and easier — so there's no excuse for not researching your topic so you can pack your copy full of interesting and persuasive supporting facts.

As Claude Hopkins once said: "Specifics sell. Generalities roll off the human understanding like water off a duck's back."

3.   The writer does not know his audience.

Just saying my audience is "pediatricians" doesn't mean you really know the audience.

What is the biggest problem keeping pediatricians up night? Do they feel treated like second-class doctors by specialty physicians such as surgeons who make more money? Why are they pediatricians — do they love kids or is there another motivation?

Unless you know how your target audience thinks ... what they believe, desire, and feel ... you won't be confident communicating with them. And that uncertainty will come across in your writing.

Aside from making sure you have a strong idea and lots of content, here are 3 simple ways to make your writing clear and easy to read:

* Use short words instead of long ones.
* Use short sentences.
* Use short paragraphs.

This last one is particularly vital: nothing turns off readers quicker than a long block of solid gray text.

Demetrius: "Short clauses should be used in forceful passages, for there is a greater force and vehemence when a lot of meaning is packed into a few words."

60

DON'T GET ENAMORED WITH WHAT'S HOT AND TRENDY IN MARKETING

These days, modern marketing is trend-driven.

Facebook ... Google Plus ... Foursquare ... Pinterest ... Instagram ... Tumblr ... content marketing ... SEO ... app ads.

These — and not good, old-fashioned ROI-driven direct marketing — are what capture the headlines in marketing trade publications today.

With each new marketing channel, a cadre of consultants almost instantly arises, ready — for a big fee — to guide clients in the use of the new medium.

Many marketers get extremely excited about new marketing trends.

I get extremely skeptical.

Here's why you might want to hesitate before taking the leap into social media or whatever flavor of the month the new media consultants are selling....

First, lots of gullible businesspeople get taken in by the newness of new media.

But where do you want to invest your marketing dollars and efforts — in what's new? Or in what's proven to work?

Once the initial excitement wears off, marketers begin to discover that some new marketing trends sound better than they perform.

GM, for instance, recently cancelled its Facebook advertising campaign ... because it wasn't producing results.

Conversely, trendy marketers often consciously avoid direct mail, landing pages, e-mail marketing, and other proven forms of direct response — precisely because they are old, not new, nor trendy.

But the best thing about "old hat" direct response marketing is that it is proven to work ... that is, to generate a positive ROI.

I find it ironic, for example, that so many social media conferences are advertised using old-fashioned paper direct mail.

Lots of articles are being written now on measuring the metrics of social media. But these metrics seem to focus on things other than dollars.

I guess it depends on your goals. Do you want to have "conversations"? Or do you want the cash register to ring?

So — should you jump on the new media bandwagon? Or eschew the trendy ... and stick with tried-and-true marketing methods?

I think the answer is to follow the Pareto Principle....

Spend 80% to 90% of your marketing budget and effort on tested direct marketing methods.

Spend 10% to 20% cautiously experimenting with new media and tracking its performance.

That way you can be in the loop without getting burned. For example....

According to an article in Direct Marketing News (5/12, p. 12), General Electric has more than 200,000 Facebook friends and more than 50,000 Twitter followers.

What does GE post on the social networks? Photos, questions, and jokes.

What do they get out of all this activity? Hundreds of "likes," comments, and mentions.

Apparently GE management thinks that getting Facebook "likes" is a worthy expenditure of time and money.

I don't.

I'd like to see proof — not conjecture, but proof — that it sells a single light bulb or refrigerator. But I have not.

One more thing:

I once worked with the marketing director of a major publisher, creating mailings for his main product, a large directory.

One year, he announced he was throwing out all our mailers and trying new "creative" mailings from a hip, young ad agency.

I'm sure you can guess what happened: the new creative bombed. And since he didn't split test against the proven old creative, sales vanished.

He was quickly fired and escorted off the premises holding a box with his family photos and other personal possessions.

The bottom line:

1. Keep using your current marketing campaigns as long as they continue to work.
2. Incrementally test new campaigns and marketing methods in small quantities — and measure performance against your "controls."
3. Lord Kelvin: "When you can measure something in numbers, then you know something about it."
4. If a trendy new marketing channel or method fails to perform in repeat tests, toss it. Spend your time elsewhere.

61

IMPROVE PERSONAL PRODUCTIVITY WITH THE PARETO PRINCIPLE

Let me share a little tip I use to stay productive in my business without getting bored or burned out.

It's a variation of the famous Pareto 80/20 principle, which says that 80% of your results come from 20% of your efforts.

Example: in Internet marketing, 80% of your online income will come from 20% of your e-list subscribers.

If you test 10 Google pay-per-click ads, 80% of the clicks will be generated by 2 of the ads.

In my freelance writing, I use the Pareto Principle this way: 80% of assignments I take are in areas where I already have experience and expertise, and 20% of my writing is in areas that are new to me.

Why this 80/20 ratio?

By spending 80% of my time (in reality my ratio is actually closer to 90/10) in familiar areas, I can work much faster because of my knowledge and experience. So my productivity soars.

By spending 10% to 20% of my time working in new areas, I stay fresh and prevent boredom from setting in.

I have come across several writers who tell me they abhor specialization and always write articles on new topics their editors assign them. In this way they are never bored.

On the other hand, they don't amortize what they learn on one topic over other assignments. So all that learning is in essence wasted, at least from a work perspective.

These generalists have to learn a new subject for every assignment. As a result, each new article takes a long time, and their output and income are limited as a result.

On the opposite end of the spectrum, I read one writer who seems to spend 100% of his time writing about an exceedingly narrow niche: silver prices.

I admire the authority with which he writes on this subject. Indeed, he is likely one of the foremost experts in the world on silver.

On the other hand, if I wrote about nothing but silver prices 40 to 60 hours a week, every week of the year, I'd be bored to tears.

I can't tell you what to do or how to spend your time at work.

But I do recommend the Pareto Principle: 80% of your time on familiar tasks and 20% of your time exploring new areas.

This strategy keeps me productive, fresh, and engaged. Maybe it can for you, too.

62

WHY INTERNET MARKETERS GIVE AWAY THEIR CONTENT FOR FREE

If you pay attention to the e-mails you get from information marketers, you notice that — in addition to selling you their content — they are also giving a lot of their content away!

You should do the same. Why?

Because if all you are doing is selling, your prospects will stop reading your e-mails.

But if you offer a combination of both free and paid content, they will stay interested and keep reading.

They will also appreciate the free stuff you give them, and pay back your generosity by ordering more from you.

What can you give away for free? Links that let your readers watch a video online free. Or listen to an audio mp3 file. Invitations to attend free Webinars. Free special reports and e-books.

The important question, however, is: What content do you give away free vs. what content do you charge for?

Many experts say that you should give away your best information! Their logic is as follows: if readers don't think your free stuff is great, they're not going to order your paid products.

The contrary school says that if you give away your best stuff, then your readers have what they need, and there's no reason to get (and pay for) additional content from you.

So ... what do you give away for free and what do you charge for?

My rule of thumb, given to me by Internet marketing consultant Wendy Montes deOca, is as follows:

Your free content tells your readers *what* to do. Your paid content tells them *how* to do it.

For example, in a recent e-mail to you, I revealed the 5 best ways to promote yourself as a freelance copywriter.

I told what the 5 methods were. But in the limited space of an e-mail, I could not possibly tell how to do each.

However, I do sell information products that teach how to do each method in great detail. And those I offer to my readers at a reasonable price.

Now, you don't always have to stick with Wendy's rule about giving away only what-to-do information. There are exceptions.

Internet marketing guru Terry Dean says, "You can also tell people how to solve a minor problem when you're selling the solution to a bigger problem."

He adds: "At times I do give the how-to away, especially when it leaves them wanting more, like when you give people how to do step one and now they need to know how to do steps two, three, and four."

WHAT'S YOUR DEFINITION
OF SUCCESS?

A few years ago, I was part of a panel of supposedly successful people speaking to a room packed with about a thousand college seniors.

Our topic: how to be successful.

When it was my turn, I asked the students: "How many of you want to be successful?"

Every hand in the room shot up.

I then asked: "Who can tell me what success is?"

Not a single hand in the room was raised.

"If you don't know what success is," I asked the students, "then how are you going to get there?"

This is the dilemma facing many people I meet today.

They desperately want to be "successful."

But when you ask them what that would mean, they either can't give you a definitive answer, or they say it would be becoming a millionaire.

They define success by how much money they have because that's how the world keeps score.

But does becoming a millionaire really make you successful?

If you won the lottery or inherited the money, you are a millionaire — but are you really a success?

If you have to do something unethical or illegal to make that much money, are you really a success?

If you work marathon days at a job that makes you miserable — same question.

That's why early in my career, I thought about what success meant to me — not what others thought success is.

And I came up with this definition: **Success is doing what I want to do ... when I want to do it ... with the people I want to work with ... and getting paid very, very well for it.**

I don't claim this is a perfect definition for success. And it may not work for you. But it works for me and many others I have shared it with in my books and lectures.

Let's break down this definition of success piece by piece....

"Success is doing what I want to do."

To me, 90% of the secret of enjoying life is having a job or business you love ... one you're so excited and enthusiastic about, you jump out of bed every morning eager to get to your office and start the day.

After all, you spend more than half your waking hours working. If you don't like work — and millions of people don't — then your days will seem to drag on almost forever. It's close to torture.

Now, the mistake people make is to believe the old saying, "Pursue your passion and the money will follow."

There are plenty of things people are passionate about (e.g., 18th century Peruvian poetry) that may be fun and interesting but have close to zero money-making potential.

The trick is to pursue an interest of yours (e.g., restoring classic cars) that people will pay for.

Aristotle said words to the effect that wherein your passion intersects with the needs of the public, therein lies your vocation.

Next, success is doing what you love "when I want to do it."

This is why 9-to-5 employment was not for me: I resented being told what to do and when to do it.

I could not abide having my freedom taken away and being subject to someone else's whims at their beck and call.

And so I quit to become a freelance copywriter.

One of the dangers of self-employment is the crisis-lull-crisis rhythm of so many businesses.

To protect yourself against the slow times, you should create multiple streams of income — some active, some passive.

I have 5 income streams: (a) copywriting, (b) consulting, (c) Internet marketing, (d) writing books, and (e) giving workshops and seminars.

That way, I am always busy. If copywriting would ever slow, as happened a few times very early in my career, I would turn to the book I had under contract or do some workshops.

The best thing is that, being self-employed, I can largely work on tasks and projects when I want to do them, not when someone else tells me to do them.

Even meetings and conference calls are scheduled by me when I want to and can do them, not when someone else commands me to.

My old friend DH says, "I don't like taking orders, and I don't like giving orders." I feel the same way.

That's why, aside from my administrative assistant, JV, I work alone. And JV is a virtual assistant, so I really am alone all day, as I prefer.

Success is doing what I want to do, when I want to do it, "with the people I want to work with."

By working diligently and consistently to build my copywriting practice, I could soon pick and choose the clients I accepted.

This way I could work only with people I like and respect — and only on projects that interest me.

If you are in a service business, figure out how much self-promotion you need to do to fill your book of business … and then do twice that amount of marketing.

This will fill your lead pipeline to overflowing and allow you to pick and choose what clients and assignments you take on.

The last part of my success formula: "getting paid very, very well."

Goal setting experts would find fault with this statement, because it does not specify a dollar amount of money.

Well, I live in an affluent neighborhood. So I decided that for me, getting paid well meant earning 4X or more per year than my average neighbor.

You may have a different money goal: higher annual earnings or the accumulation of a net worth of a certain dollar amount; i.e. a million bucks.

That's a valuable and laudable goal, but it simply isn't part of my personal success definition. But by all means, if you want it to be part of your success definition, go for it.

One other thing....

I have a litmus test for your definition of success, and it's simple: Does it allow you to live comfortably? Does it make you happy?

If you can say yes, then you are successful. At least in my eyes. And I hope in yours, too.

64

INFORMATION MARKETING: BEYOND E-BOOKS

There are countless Internet information marketers out there who only sell e-books.

Are you one?

On the surface, e-books are the ideal information product to sell online.

After all, you can easily outsource their creation — eliminating a lot of labor on your part.

As an electronic product, e-books have no printing, shipping, inventory, or handling costs. It costs you close to zero to fulfill your orders!

Yet there is a problem with e-books that can limit the potential profits of your Internet information marketing business: the relatively low price you can charge for e-books.

My e-books are priced from $19 to $59, with most selling for around $29.

You've got to sell an awful lot of e-books to make the thousands of dollars we are promised by the "get rich quick online" promoters.

The solution is to go beyond e-books and produce other types of information products that command higher prices.

I can think of at least 6 right off the bat:

1. Audio-visual media.

    I sell albums of 2 to 4 audio CDs for about $100 each. A set of 2 DVDs also goes for around $100. If your subject is more specialized, or you have more than half a dozen CDs or DVDs in the package, you can charge substantially more.

2. Multimedia.

    The price of the audio or video product jumps incrementally when you add elements in other media to make it a multimedia product — for example, mix audio CDs with DVDs, or add a PDF or printed manual.

    The packaging also influences the price. You can command a price of several hundred dollars for a thick printed manual in a 3-ring binder with plastic sleeves holding audio CDs and DVDs.

3. Subscription Web sites.

    People will pay $29 to $79 a month or more for access to a content-rich subscription Web site, also called a membership site.

    It's profitable because once they buy, their credit card is pinged for that amount every month until they instruct you to unsubscribe them. A $49 a month site membership brings you nearly $600 in income a year.

4. Coaching.

    Webinars can be free or paid, but offer some Webinars mixed in with some live group calls, and you can call it coaching. If you have a dozen students paying $100 per month each, that's $1,200 per month.

5. Consulting.

Some info product buyers may want more individual and hands-on advice and help from you. Consulting rates go from $100 to $500 an hour and up.

6. Software.

Can you think of an application that would be useful or entertaining to your customers? You can find freelance programmers to create it at reasonable cost. Software can sell either for a one-time purchase price, a licensing fee, or a monthly subscription.

If you are strictly an e-book seller, I advise you to expand into some of these other media. That way you'll have a more complete product line with varying price points.

Result: you'll have low-priced e-books to entice new customers and for repeat sales to existing e-book buyers. But you'll also be able to sell a percentage of your e-book buyers on more expensive products in the $100 to $500 range and up.

65

FIVE PROVEN STRATEGIES FOR GETTING CLIENTS

The other day, an interviewer asked me, "What are your top 5 strategies for getting clients?" Here's what I told him:

1. Create a content-rich Web site.

    Put up a Web site on your services. Then load it up with free content. The content positions you as an expert in your field. And it gets visitors to spend a lot of time on your site. I have dozens of free articles and free special reports posted on my site.

2. SEO.

    Optimize your Web site for search engines using key words related to your service. This will bring a lot of traffic to your site. Have a form on the site where visitors can register and tell you about their needs. This will convert traffic into sales leads.

3. Start an e-newsletter.

   Write and publish a monthly online newsletter. Create a sign-up page and drive traffic to it using e-mail marketing, Google Ad Words, and other traffic generation methods. Work to build your subscriber list from hundreds to thousands. The more prospects who see your newsletter, the better known you become.

4. Write articles.

   Writing and publishing how-to articles on your specialty further positions you as an expert in your topic. You can post the published articles on your Web site to add content and impress visitors. You can also use article reprints as mailers. For more information on how to write articles for both print magazines as well as online newsletters, click here now:

   www.getfamouswritingarticles.com

5. Give talks.

   Find local chapters of associations to which your prospects belong. Offer to give a talk at a lunch or dinner meeting. Since these local chapters don't pay speakers, they are always looking for someone to give a presentation for free. Volunteer to do it.

   If you give a good talk, some prospects in the audience will become interested in hiring you. Offer a free article reprint or tip sheet in exchange for their business cards. Then follow up by e-mail or phone.

Here's a tip: record your speech. Duplicate the talk on audio CDs and mail them with your brochure to prospects who request information on your services. Post the audio as an mp3 on your site and send your e-newsletter subscribers a link where they can hear it.

If you want to avoid travel or are nervous about speaking live before a group, give and record an audio tele-conference on your topic. Invite your online subscribers to attend for free. Post-conference, make the audio recording available as an mp3 and CD.

66

CONSUMERS LOVE FREEBIES

My local mall has a food court with some pretty good places to eat.

The busiest by far is Chick-Fil-A.

Why?

Because an employee is usually standing in front of the counter, giving away samples.

It's a well-known and very simple marketing technique that many marketers ignore: you can sell more of your product by giving some away.

It works because free is one of the most powerful words in the English language ... and people love free stuff.

In fact, one of my friends made his fortune in mail order by publishing and selling through direct response ads a small book titled, "A Few Thousand of the Best Free Things in America."

It's great fun to go through the book and send for all the free stuff!

One of my subscribers, SJ, writes: "Subscribers often expect free stuff as a right, rather than a good turn."

That's been my experience. Getting free stuff has become the expected standard, not a rare bonus.

If you sell everything and give away nothing, your readers will see you as mercenary rather than concerned about their welfare.

No one like being ripped off. No one likes feeling that their vendor is squeezing them for every dime they have.

That's why I price most of my products under $50 while my competitors charge hundreds of dollars — or even thousands — for their products covering similar topics.

And every product I sell comes with at least one free bonus.

I also give away stuff in my freelance copywriting practice.

For instance, I routinely give away an audio CD on copywriting that sells for $29.

In some cases, I also give away a copy of one of my books as a gift.

Here are some suggestions for strengthening your marketing results by giving away stuff for free:

- Give away a bonus with every product you sell.
- Make bonus reports generous. Mine average 50 pages of content. Yours can be shorter.
- Offer freebies to your e-list; e.g. free Webinars, videos, special reports, e-books.
- When you have a customer complaint, resolve it and then give the customer a free e-book or report to make up for their inconvenience.
- If you publish an e-newsletter, make it content-rich, not just a sales vehicle.
- Answer subscriber questions about your products by e-mail or phone.

67

MOTIVATING CONSUMERS WITH THE 4 DS OF MARKETING

You know that for your marketing to work, it must tap into a powerful emotion the buyer is experiencing.

The emotions most commonly targeted in copy: greed, guilt, fear, and exclusivity.

Of course there are many others: love, hate, envy, joy, empathy, benevolence.

I've identified 4 other emotions that work for a wide variety of offers but especially for business opportunity and money-making offers.

They are desire, dissatisfaction, disappointment, and despair. I call them the "4 Ds."

There are many similarities between the Ds, but subtle differences, too:

1. Desire.

Prospects who respond to business opportunity and money-making offers want something.

Not just a little. They crave its possession.

For some prospects, the desire is for money or material objects — a boat, vacation home, luxury car — and they need money to own it.

For many, it's the difference that money can make in their lives: the ability to run your own business, quit your 9-to-5 job, or get rid of money worries for good.

Others desire the security and peace of mind they think financial independence will bring.

Promising the fulfillment of the prospect's prominent desire is a powerful way to entice him to pull the trigger and invest in your product.

2. Dissatisfaction.

Countless individuals slog through life, unhappy and dissatisfied with their lot.

They want something better, but are often unclear on what that would be or how to achieve it.

In business opportunity marketing, our selling proposition is that we will help you make the money you need to live the life you want to live.

In self-help and spiritual marketing, the promise is often to show you how to be happy and fulfilled by who you are and what you have.

Dissatisfaction is a potent emotion to tap into. Dissatisfaction is emotional pain.

People act mainly for two reasons: to attain pleasure and avoid pain. Of these, the avoidance of pain can be stronger than the attainment of pleasure.

Another way to put it is that people act for only two reasons: to gain reward and avoid punishment.

3. Disappointment.

What's the difference between dissatisfaction and disappointment?

Dissatisfaction means the prospect has a problem he has not solved or a situation he cannot resolve — for example, he wants to own a BMW but can't afford it.

Disappointment is more specific. It means the prospect has tried to solve the problem or resolve the situation — and it hasn't worked out.

The disappointed prospect is wary of marketing claims. That makes him highly skeptical and difficult to sell.

It's far easier to market to prospects who have had some degree of success solving their problem and want more help.

As a copywriter, for example, some potential clients tell me how they have hired an endless string of copywriters and all of them have failed.

When I hear that, I run for the hills. I'd rather have a client who hires and works well with her copywriters.

4. Despair.

Despair means the prospect's situation is so dire, it is emotionally painful.

The prospect feels no one can help him and there is no hope.

The best approach here is to prove that what you offer does in fact work and has worked for many of your customers.

Testimonials, case studies, and YouTube videos are three obvious marketing tactics for proving your claims. There are others; e.g., show images of checks you have received as a result of using your money-making system.

You may think the 4 Ds — desire, dissatisfaction, disappointment, and despair — are too negative.

But negative marketing can work. Fear is a powerful motivator. It's not universally right for every marketing campaign. But next time you're formulating your promotional strategy, see if you can build a message around one of the 4 Ds.

68

WHY YOU CAN'T DO EVERYTHING

Though I normally dislike business jargon, there's one term that I actually like: "bandwidth."

In the New York Review of Books (9/26/13, p. 47), Cass Sunstein writes: "The central idea of bandwidth is that people have the capacity to focus on, and to promote and implement, only a subset of the universe of good ideas."

As a result, smart people often don't do things that make sense to do — not because they don't agree that these things are sensible, but because they lack the bandwidth to investigate them.

Your bandwidth is a function of 4 different factors:

1. Time: There are 24 hours in a day and not one minute more, and if you sleep 8 hours a day, that leaves only 16 hours … hardly the infinite amount of time all of us could really use.

2. Attention: The human mind has a limited attention span. Only so many things at a time can hold our attention, and the attention we seem willing to give to any one of them is limited.

3. Energy: Your physical and mental energy are limited. And they diminish with age, as does patience.

4. Priority: Yes, there are a lot of good ideas out there. But not everyone can be first.

Based on these criteria, here are a few "bandwidth bandits" that can rapidly diminish your already limited bandwidth and further reduce the amount of tasks you can handle:

- When you waste time, as most people do, you erode your bandwidth. This is why I am such a fanatic about not wasting time.

- The more tired you are, the less energy you have, and the lower your bandwidth. This is why getting a good night's sleep before each new work day is such a priority with me — so much so that I refuse to participate in activities requiring me to stay up past midnight on a weekday.

- Lack of priorities means you are consuming your limited supply of bandwidth on the wrong tasks.

- As Brian Tracy preaches, successful people have goals. Without specific goals on which to focus your attention, it weakens — and this reduces your bandwidth.

In my experience, a lot of the people I deal with simply do not understand the concept of bandwidth — or at least, the limitations of my personal bandwidth.

For instance, subscriber BK writes and suggests I am an ignoramus for not knowing or using certain marketing techniques on my Web site.

What BK does not understand is that I am well aware of these techniques. I agree they are valuable. So BK does not really know anything about Web marketing that I don't know, though she mistakenly and smugly believes she does.

But, because of my limited bandwidth, I have not implemented BK's marketing suggestions: I have too many other things to think of and do that are more important.

I am deluged with people asking why I have not produced a particular product ... or used a marketing tactic ... or read an important book ... or attended a valuable marketing conference ... or tried a healthful dietary supplement.

My answer is always the same: "I have 5,000 things to do," I tell them, "but I only have time today to do 3,500." So some things that are worthwhile are going to fall by the wayside.

As a businessperson, you need to realize that your customers and clients have limited bandwidth, too.

A freelance copywriter called me in a panic. Turns out she got what she thought was a great lead from LD, a potential client. They had a good initial conversation. But after that, she heard nothing despite repeat follow-ups.

"Did I do something wrong?" she implored me. "Was my price too high? Do I have bad breath?"

Again, the answer is bandwidth. When LD called her, the copywriting project was no doubt a hot priority.

But priorities shift in the blink of an eye. When she followed up with LD days later, the project was most likely not his top priority any longer, and he lacked the bandwidth to engage with her. This happens in vendor/prospect relationships all the time.

Counterintuitive though it may sound at first, according to an article by David Brooks in the New York Times (7/7/11), poorer people have even less bandwidth than the middle class.

Says Brooks: "Poorer people have to think hard about a million things that affluent people don't. They have to make complicated trade-offs when buying a carton of milk: If I buy milk, I can't afford orange juice. They have to decide which utility not to pay."

Recently, JR wrote me to complain about a broken link to a product offer on my Web site, which he found annoying because it wasted the massive amount of time it took him to clink on the link and discover it to be not working.

I told JR that I have 5,000 things to do, but I only have time to do 3,500 of them. So some things, like regularly scanning the hundreds of pages on my site for broken links, are going to fall by the wayside.

He replied, "Can't you get a virtual assistant to do that for you?" Well, JR, thanks for the brilliant suggestion. Gee, I never thought of that!

Of course I have a virtual assistant! The problem, JR, is that she too had bandwidth limitations: 2,000 things to do but time for only 1,500 of them. And continually scanning my site for dead links is so low a priority, it is not even on her radar.

SEVEN TIPS FOR GETTING
YOUR BOOK PUBLISHED

I have been coming up with ideas for books and selling them to traditional publishing houses continually since 1981.

My track record so far: 80 published books and counting.

Has anything changed in the process of selling your book to a major publisher in the last 30 years or so?

Oh, yes indeed:

1. Many nonfiction books have been sold based on a clever or useful repackaging of known information.

    Example: Dummies and Idiot's Guide books convey useful but known information with unique packaging and format. (I should know. I've written one of each.)

    Today, editors are increasingly demanding unique information: innovative techniques or ideas that have not appeared in other books before. Fresh packaging and format alone are not enough.

2. If you do not have an active Web site on the topic of your proposed book, your chances of selling it to a big publishing house are slim. Editors are now asking potential authors to provide Web analytic reports showing their Web site hits and unique visits.

   If your Web site has little traffic, you are in trouble. Therefore, I urge you to optimize your site for the key word(s) used in your book title.

3. Blog. Having a blog can get you a book deal, and not having a blog can impede you from obtaining one.

   One major publisher just asked me for my blog stats, which I must confess I don't ever look at.

   Another gave me a $20,000 book contract based on one of my blog posts!

4. Social media. The same major publisher who asked for my blog stats also wanted to know the number of LinkedIn contacts, Facebook friends, and Twitter followers I had — three more statistics I never pay the least bit of attention to. But now I will have to start.

   This is a bad trend for writers like me who are not active participants in social networks.

5. List size. Do you publish an e-newsletter? How many subscribers do you have?

   A monthly or more frequently published e-zine with 50,000 or more subscribers is enticing to book publishers; they want to know you have a built-in audience you can easily and cheaply reach online.

6. Book sales. What other books have you written and how many copies have sold?

   You can't hide weak sales; the new publisher can easily find this out from your existing publishers. If your last book went into the toilet in sales, publishers are likely to stay away from your next one.

7. What is your "platform?" How well known are you to the potential buyers of your book? How many of them are there?

If Dr. Oz wants to write a health book, it will get published because he is on television. If you want to write a health book, good luck.

The bottom line: it is getting more and more difficult to sell your book idea to a mainstream publisher today.

You need more than a good book idea or even a good book. You need a reputation in your niche, a large built-in audience for your book, and a cost-effective way to reach them.

70

DO THIS BEFORE E-MAILING AFFILIATE OFFERS TO YOUR LIST

Everybody tells you the same thing: broaden your product line by offering "OPP" (Other People's Products) as their affiliate.

It seems easy: just run the e-mail promotion they give you to your e-list, sit back, let them handle the sales, and collect a nice commission check.

But it's not quite that simple. I have been burned several times by not performing my "due diligence" on any affiliate offer a partner or colleague asked me to promote to my e-list.

Here are 5 things you can do to ensure that your affiliate promotions won't displease or upset your valued subscribers:

1. Read the e-mail.

    Don't just distribute the promotional e-mail the marketer gives you to your list. Read it carefully.

On one recent promotion, the marketer gave me an e-mail to send to my e-list. It was written in my voice and talked about the success I had achieved using the product.

I had reviewed the product but had not started to use it yet. So it was a complete lie. And I don't lie to my list. Others apparently don't have a problem making up stuff, but I do.

2. Read the landing page.

Read the entire landing page that the e-mail links to. Make sure you are comfortable with the wording and the content.

Recently I read the e-mail my joint venture partner gave me to send out but not the landing page it linked to. Turns out, that landing page was full of typos and errors, and several of my subscribers chastised me for it.

3. Review the product.

I am often asked to endorse a book I have not read or even seen. When I tell the joint venture partner I can't do it, they often offer to send me the intro and chapter one.

Sorry, that's not good enough. If I don't read the whole thing word for word, I at least need to skim through it. Otherwise, how do I know what I am recommending to my list is any good.

4. Consider the source.

Different Internet marketers have different degrees of ethics and promotional practices.

I pride myself on being an ethical and honest marketer. Many other online entrepreneurs out there use a far greater degree of hype in marketing than I do.

When I sell one of their products as an affiliate, I am in effect endorsing them. If my subscribers have a problem with me endorsing that marketer, they will surely let me know it.

5. Make sure you understand the offer.

Recently I offered a marketer's inexpensive special report to my list as an affiliate.

6. I didn't realize the marketer would focus on up-selling report buyers immediately to a very expensive product, and some of my subscribers were offended by the up-sell.

   In their minds, your subscribers don't differentiate between your marketing, products, and offers and those you promote as an affiliate.

   Therefore, products you promote as an affiliate must be as useful, valuable, and ethical as your own — otherwise, you will have unhappy customers on your hands.

71

HOW TO CUT DOWN
ON REFUND REQUESTS

Many Internet marketers I know hate refund requests.

"My product is great," they think. "Anybody who would return it must be a boob."

Not necessarily. In fact, there are 6 perfectly legitimate reasons why some of your customers will return your product for a refund:

1. They change their minds.

    I had one customer return my Internet Marketing Retirement Plan CDs. Reason? After listening to them, he decided the business was not for him.

2. They've heard it before.

    The customer has already bought 9 programs on this topic and yours is the 10th. If there's nothing new in yours, he may return it for refund.

3. They didn't understand what they were buying.

I had one customer scream at me, "These discs won't play in my car's CD player."

"That's because, as it clearly says on my Web site, they are DVDs, not audio CDs," I replied.

This was clearly stated on the landing page. But not everybody reads every word of your copy. So he could easily have missed it.

I also have e-book buyers complain that they have not received a hardcover or paperback book ... when it clearly says "e-book" in my sales copy.

4. They don't like your media.

Every week people complain to me that they don't like audio CDs, DVDs, and e-books, and why don't I produce my program in a format they do like.

One solution for audio and DVD products: transcribe them and sell a PDF of the transcription (or give it away as a free bonus with purchase of the CDs or DVDs).

5. They think the material is out of date.

On the Internet, any information product with a copyright date older than a couple of years is seen by some buyers as automatically out of date. Ridiculous, but that's how they feel.

6. They think your product is of inferior quality.

One customer requesting a refund told me, "Your product is worth the $29 you charge for it, but not more than that.

People don't want their money's worth. They want more than their money's worth.

So how do you cut way down on your refund rates and product returns? Here are a few suggestions....

- Update your information products at least every year or two, preferably more often. That way, they reflect your latest thinking and knowledge as well as industry developments.

- For these revised editions, update the copyright date to reflect the latest edition.

- Offer your information in multiple formats — print, audio, video.
- Make it clear on the landing page whether a particular product is an e-book, audio CD album, DVD set, subscription Web site, whatever.
- Organize your material by chapter, module, disk, track, whatever. The better organized your information, the more valuable to the customer.
- Give a longer guarantee (e.g., 90 days) rather than a shorter guarantee. The longer the customer has the product, the less likely he is to return it.
- In the beginning or introduction to the product, give your bio and credentials as an expert in the field.
- Collect testimonials about the product from satisfied customers and post them on your landing page.
- Sales copy should accurately describe the product. If the product doesn't live up to its hype, you'll get more refund requests.
- Charge a fair price. If the customer perceives that the price is higher than the value received, she will ask for a refund.

72

HOW TO TREAT YOUR BEST CUSTOMERS ... AND YOUR WORST

There are two types of customers you must pay special attention to in your business: (1) the excellent customer and (2) the extremely unhappy customer.

The excellent customer is someone who can't stop buying your products, has been easy to service, and raves about you to everyone he knows.

Only now they are asking for something a bit out of the ordinary — and have created a special situation that must be handled.

Since satisfied customers are your most important asset, you want to go to extremes to keep these extremely happy customers happy.

For instance, one wanted to substitute one of my e-books for a free bonus report I was offering — something we don't normally give away.

But he had bought tons from us, so I happily gave it to him.

He was so happy, he immediately bought yet another product from me.

The other type of customer you want to handle personally and with great care is the extremely unhappy customer.

Reason: unhappy customers tell other people. The more unhappy they become, the more people they complain about you to — and the louder they say it.

In the good old days, an unhappy customer told maybe 5 or 10 other people.

But with social networking, they can tell thousands with a few key strokes and mouse clicks.

I had a problem with a product I bought online, but could get no satisfaction from the seller, who refused to even take my call.

So I wrote about it on my blog.

Within 24 hours, the marketer called, apologized profusely, immediately fixed the problem, and begged me to remove the post from my blog.

Despite this newfound power consumers enjoy online, many Internet businesses treat their customers poorly.

I hear complaints all the time from people. They tell me they bought a product online, but when they called about returning it, the Internet marketer became abrupt and rude.

Or they tell me about Internet marketers who flat out refuse, on the flimsiest of excuses, to honor their money-back guarantees.

I hear horror stories of Internet marketers who recruit affiliates, let them generate sales, and then don't send commission checks.

A lot of consumers are frustrated that Internet marketers are so darn inaccessible.

I mean, if you have a problem with your phone line, you can call the phone company and eventually can get a real person on the phone, right?

But when you want to complain to an Internet marketer, more often than not there is no mailing address or phone number.

And when you send them an e-mail, you get a response from a robot — an auto-responder — and not a live human being.

The e-mail tells you how busy the marketer is. Sometimes it promises a return call from a person ... which usually never comes.

I have heard of Internet marketers who blow their stacks at customers — particularly older customers — who aren't that computer literate and have trouble opening and reading an e-book or downloading and listening to a Webinar.

They may frustrate you and try your patience, but think about how frustrated they must feel. They just bought great content from you, and now they can't access it.

The collective sigh of all the Internet customers who despair at the treatment they receive from Internet marketers is palpable.

Is this how you're treating some or all of your customers? If so, something a speaker told me can serve as your new customer service policy....

At a recent meeting of the Ethical Culture Society of Bergen County, this speaker said that a precept of the organization is: "Every person deserves to be treated fairly and kindly."

This is great advice especially if you are an Internet marketer. Because from what I see, there are many Internet marketers who don't follow this rule.

"But," you argue, "I can't personally respond to each complaint. That's what I have an auto-responder or an assistant for."

First of all, assuming your products are a good value, you're not getting all that many complaints to begin with.

Second of all, you probably could respond to all of them, if you wanted to.

SL, a major catalog marketer, writes a personal note of apology — and sends it along with a small gift — whenever his rather large catalog company gets an unhappy customer.

If SL can do it, you and I can do it too.

But let's say you are busy, and can personally respond to only a fraction of the complaints you get. What should you do?

Well, I hired a part-time assistant in my Internet marketing business, and it's her job to handle all complaints and special requests, which she does with sensitivity and common sense.

However, I see all the complaints and special requests first, and I pick certain ones to handle personally. These are from the two types of customers I mentioned at the beginning of this essay — the extremely unhappy ones and the valuable repeat customers who spend a small fortune with you.

Every person deserves to be treated fairly and kindly. Are you treating every customer and prospect fairly? Do you do it angrily or kindly?

One more thing: add unadvertised grace periods to your money-back guarantees.

For instance, if you have a 90-day money-back guarantee and the customer returns your product on day 92, should you give him his money back anyway?

Yes, because you want to treat him fairly and kindly ... just like you'd want to be treated when returning an item to a store.

And if you treat your customers fairly and kindly, they will deal with you in the same way.

73

GET RICH IN YOUR NICHE

The most important piece of advice I ever give anyone — whether they are a copywriter, consultant, writer, Internet marketer, or retail merchant — is to specialize.

Find an under-served niche that needs what you are selling … and become the leading guru in that space.

When I give this reply, the other person invariably says, "I want to specialize, but I don't know which niche to pick."

The possibilities are endless:

- My friend DK specializes in showing small business owners how to rank their Web sites #1 in Google for local search.
- FG teaches marketing and customer service to owners of self-storage facilities.
- GG sells video training programs teaching optometrists how to better manage their practices.

- Another info marketer, "Mr. Excel," teaches people how to become proficient with Excel.
- DP shows people how to deal with and care for a relative who is bipolar.
- PF creates marketing programs for hearing aid dealers.

Fortunately, I've developed a simple process that can help you identify and select your niche in about 20 minutes.

To begin with, here are the 10 questions you should ask yourself when determining the niche in which you will specialize.

As you think of the answers, write them down on index cards:

- What do I like?
- What am I interested in?
- What am I good at?
- What do I have an aptitude for?
- What is my education?
- What do I know?
- What is my experience?
- What have I accomplished?
- Which of the above areas has the least competition?
- Which of the above areas pays high rates?

For the above categories, write down as many items under each category as you possibly can on index cards, one per card.

Once you have completed your lists, look them over, and set aside in a separate stack the cards for any items that look like possible niches.

Next, pick the five most interesting potential niches. Put these cards in order of preference.

Now look at this list of your top five items. Chances are that one or two of these subjects are things people routinely pay to learn about or need help with.

Pick one and you've found your niche. As Aristotle said, "Where your passions intersect with the needs of the public, therein lies your vocation."

What if none of the five items on your list is appealing to you as a niche? Pick the next best five items from your index cards and repeat the process until you have a niche you are enthusiastic about.

Your niche can be broad or narrow. Broad niches have lots of potential customers but also lots of well-established competitors. Narrow niches have far fewer potential customers, but little or no significant competition.

As a rule, the narrower the niche, the better your business. We live in an age of specialization, and people want to hire specialists. They prefer products and services that reflect knowledge of what they perceive to be their unique situations and problems.

In information marketing, the more specialized your topic, the more you can charge for your book or report. A course on "designing distillation towers" can command 100 times the price of a book on "leadership."

The worry in a narrow niche is not enough customers to support your business. But you really don't need that many to make a very nice living.

The desire to have a huge mailing list is a laudable goal but not necessary for success. If you have an e-list of only 10,000 subscribers who spend an average of $100 a year, you'll gross a million dollars annually.

Most experts advise choosing a niche that you are passionate about. I think it's more important to choose a niche you won't become bored with. After all, you'll be living in it for a long time, and to me there's almost nothing worse than sitting at your PC every day to do work that bores you.

Become a more active participant in your niche. For instance, if your niche is tropical fish-keeping (see my site www.aquariumdetective.com), join and become active in your local aquarium hobbyist club.

People buy from people who are like them — who act the same, believe the same things, live the same lifestyle, or have the same interests.

When you are an active participant in your niche, you can talk more authentically to your market — a crowd of people passionately interested in that topic.

Listen to the problems, concerns, and interests of other active participants in your niche. Then create information products that address those areas.

74

THERE'S NO SUBSTITUTE FOR REAL-WORLD EXPERIENCE

Each month, I am besieged by nice, well-meaning folk who desperately desire to be writers, consultants, coaches, speakers, and information marketers.

Many of these people actually have quite a bit of talent for writing, consulting, coaching, speaking, and authoring information products.

Yet most will not succeed for a single common reason....

They have nothing to teach, write, or speak *about*.

You see this all the time....

- Marketing consultants who have never held a corporate marketing job or worked at an ad agency or created a single winning marketing campaign.
- Numerous sales trainers who were either mediocre salesmen or never sold anything at all.

- Business opportunity marketers who have never actually done the businesses that they write and talk about.
- Financial newsletter editors who haven't made a dime in the market in years.
- Internet marketers who sell e-books written by freelance ghostwriters who knew nothing about the topic and just researched it online with Google.

To succeed as a writer, speaker, consultant, coach, and especially as an Internet info marketer, you need just 2 things: (a) the ability to write, speak, consult, or coach and (b) something to write, speak, consult, or coach about.

To be fair, you also need to know how to (c) market, promote, and sell yourself to get leads, customers, and sales.

Lots of people have the (a) and (c) can be learned, but too many lack (b) — a subject to write about.

RS, author of books and newsletters on gold and gold investing, once told me: If you can gain specialized knowledge, you will never go broke.

The best way to gain this knowledge is as a participant in or practitioner of the skill or specialized field you want to write about.

People believed RS when he recommended investing in a particular gold stock, because before he edited a newsletter on gold stocks, he spent 3 decades as a mining consultant.

Some wanna-be gurus decide they will master a field by reading about it and studying it, and neglect to actually participate in it.

That's a mistake.

Book learning is important, but there are limits to how far it can take you, and it is no substitute for real-world experience.

For instance, years ago, I signed up at a local adult education program to take a course in mail order.

At the time I had a small mail order business, and I had been in direct marketing for decades … but I am always reading and taking classes to see what extra knowledge I can pick up.

When the class started, it was obvious the instructor — a business teacher at a local community college — was reading from a textbook and had absolutely zero experience in and knowledge of mail order.

The class bombarded her with questions which she could not answer. Since I had identified myself when the teacher took attendance, I was trapped into answering them and pretty much teaching the rest of the class — not what I wanted.

I once read an article by professional speaker Mike Aun in which he talked about the fact that in addition to being a speaker, he ran a successful insurance agency.

He asserted that no one should be a full-time professional speaker; having a real business gave him the knowledge and content he needed to deliver in his talks.

I agree with Aun. I am frequently asked when I give a seminar on copywriting whether I just give seminars or do I still write copy.

I am proud to reply that I am an active participant in every area (copywriting, Internet marketing, book publishing, freelance writing) that I teach others through my how-to writing and speaking.

I don't see how I could do otherwise. Active participation keeps your skills sharp and your knowledge level current.

It also gives you a living laboratory in which to test out your ideas to make sure your advice works in the real world.

And, it establishes your credibility with the audience or reader.

I once heard a speaker tell a group of aspiring speakers to read books on their topics an hour a day every day for a full year.

"If you do, you will be an expert on your topic and qualified to teach it to others," the speaker said.

To which I reply: no, you won't.

You will have a theoretical knowledge of your topic.

But you will lack the confidence and depth of knowledge that having actual experience in a process, skill, or activity gives you.

The other danger of learning only by reading instead of doing is that a lot of how-to writers don't know their subjects that well ... and frequently give wrong advice.

If you have no real-world experience and haven't tried the methods you teach, you have no way of knowing whether they work or not.

Writing, speaking, and consulting about a topic you know thoroughly is easier — and a lot more fun — than trying to fake your way through a subject in which you are barely conversant.

When you're a true expert, your reports, e-books, and other information products seem to fly out of your PC with lightning speed and always ring true to your customers.

In addition, your customers will recognize and praise your genuine expertise, giving a big boost to your self-esteem and ego.

Plus, as a true expert, you are light years ahead of your competitors who only know your topic through second-hand research or minimal real-world experience.

Therefore you enjoy a significant competitive edge both in the quality of your products and services and the effectiveness of your marketing.

And it all starts with knowing your topic inside and out.

75

TIME TO STOP READING AND START DOING

KJ, like so many of my subscribers these days, wants to get into Internet marketing.

But she told me in an e-mail that she feels frustrated and unable to move forward.

"Where should I begin?" KJ asked me. "What was your tipping point to online success?"

My answer to KJ was: "The tipping point in Internet marketing success is to stop reading about it and stop talking about it and actually start doing it."

I'm not saying you shouldn't learn something about Internet marketing before you start.

I am saying you do not need to learn everything about Internet marketing before you start.

It's simply Michael Masterson's success principle of "Ready, Fire, Aim" in action.

And it's especially true in Internet marketing.

There is an oppressive mountain of boot camps ... courses ... seminars ... workbooks ... coaching programs ... DVDs ... Web sites ... audio CDs ... e-books ... reports ... and other "how to get rich quick on the Internet" material out there. (I sell some of it myself.)

Aspiring Internet marketers quite sensibly buy and study this material in preparation for the day when they start their own fledgling Internet marketing business.

Unfortunately, for the vast majority, that day never comes.

They get so caught up in reading and talking about Internet marketing, that they forget to actually do Internet marketing.

And so they never graduate beyond the student phase and move into the real world.

The problem with this, of course, is that their knowledge remains theoretical and never becomes applied knowledge ... and, they never make a dime from it.

To be sure, many people really enjoy reading how-to business books and studying marketing.

If you're in that group ... and all you want is a pleasant, intellectually stimulating hobby to pass the time ... well, nothing wrong with that.

Lots of people read and study for nothing other than the pleasure of learning.

But KJ — and, I'm guessing, you also — wants something more from studying Internet marketing than just entertainment.

Specifically, you want to start and build a home-based Internet marketing business.

And by doing so, earn thousands of dollars a year in extra income.

To do that, you have to stop just studying Internet marketing ... and actually start doing Internet marketing.

Every day, I hear this from one of my readers:

"I'm almost ready to start my online business. I just have to finish reading Mr. X's book and taking Mr. Y's coaching program."

My advice to them is to forget about X and Y.

More than likely, you've already bought and read a ton of material on Internet marketing.

At this point, you will learn much more through real-life trial and error than buying more education.

KJ also told me that another thing holding her back was that she was a "rookie with no capital."

I have news for KJ.

Everyone who is successful in Internet marketing today was a rookie no farther back than ten to fifteen years ago ... and many much more recently.

So being a rookie doesn't stop you.

As for "no capital" being a disadvantage — it simply isn't.

Internet marketing is one of the least capital-intensive business opportunities on the planet.

You can create and launch your first product online for only a few hundred dollars.

If you truly don't have even a few hundred dollars to launch your first product, start by selling someone else's product for an affiliate commission.

KJ also told me that she knows "a little bit about everything in Internet marketing."

It's good to be so well versed. But most of us aren't.

There are dozens of techniques for making money selling products and services online.

But to get started, you don't have to know all of them — or even most of them.

In fact, you only need 3 things to get started in Internet marketing:

1. People to sell to — either visitors to your Web site (traffic), your e-list of online subscribers, or e-lists owned by joint venture (JV) partners.
2. A product to sell them — either your own or a product produced by a JV partner.

3. A way to sell it to them — usually e-mail marketing messages driving potential buyers to a dedicated landing page or micro-site.

So when is the best time to start your new Internet marketing business? Quite simply, it's today. And here's how....

First, decide to work on your new business venture at least 5 days a week, at least an hour a day.

Second, make a list of 10 things you need to do to get the business off the ground.

When your hour to work on your business arrives, immediately start working on item #1 on your top 10 things-to-do list.

Spend all your business start-up time working on that item until either it is done or you can't work on it any more that day.

Then move to #2 and repeat the process, going down the list until the top 10 items are done.

As for spending more time studying Internet marketing....

If you know everything you need to know about Internet marketing from your studies, more power to you.

If you don't, keep studying ... but on your own time, not during your daily hour devoted to starting up your business.

Yes, there's always more to learn. But you'll learn it as you go along. And because you'll be doing Internet marketing and not just reading about it, the lessons will stick better and be more meaningful to you.

Not to mention much more profitable.

76

DO YOU BURN WITH THE ENVY OF OTHERS?

I know a lot of rich people ... a slew of hard-driving individuals whose wealth and accomplishments put the rest of the population to shame.

I've also spent a lot of my life — too much, in fact — comparing myself to them ... and of course, coming up short.

So I'm not going to do it any more.

And neither should you.

If you judge yourself only in comparison to others — who they are, what they have, what they've done — you can always find someone who outperforms you in any given area.

As Max Ehrmann observed in his 1923 essay Desiderata, "There will always be those both greater and lesser than you."

We obsess about those who are "greater" — and feel bad that we don't measure up to their success and accomplishments.

Psychologists call this unhealthy obsession "compare despair."

So what can you do about it?

To begin with, stop comparing yourself to others ... because unless you're Bill Gates, there's always someone who makes more money than you.

Unless you're George Clooney or Jessica Alba, there's always someone either more famous — or better looking — or both.

So quit worrying about how you stack up against other people.

Instead, figure out what's important to you — helping others in need, writing good books or great copy, being a terrific parent, becoming a guru in your industry or market niche, or giving your clients a level of service they can't get anywhere else.

Then, when you know you've made the absolute best effort you can in pursuit of these objectives ... take a minute to feel good about yourself.

After all, you deserve it.

77

WRITE LIKE THEY TALK

We copywriters are taught to write conversational copy. Many marketers erroneously think "conversational copy" means "write like you talk." But what it really means is "write the way your *prospects* talk."

A public radio station in my area, featuring eclectic rock and pop, sent me a fundraising letter. It began: "Dear Neighbor: I know you are a savvy media consumer."

Now, I don't know about you, but if you ask me why I listen to the radio, I would not say because I am a savvy media consumer; I'd say, "I like music."

Here's my rewrite for the fundraising letter lead:

"Dear Fellow Music Lover: Do you ever wish, when you turn on the radio, that they'd play OUR music?"

While my rewrite hasn't been tested against the original, I believe it's an improvement, for two reasons.

First, it talks about something the reader cares about: hearing music I like when I turn on the radio.

Second, it establishes an empathy-based bond through a common interest between the reader and the writer: that we share similar musical tastes — which is why I said "our" music instead of "your" music.

"In most cases, you should write in a conversational, intimate voice," says copywriter Susanna K. Hutcheson. "You should talk as if you're having coffee with the reader and use her language. Many copywriters, and just about all people who write their own copy, don't understand the concept of writing in the language of the reader. It's truly an art."

Is there any situation where you should use language other than conversational copy? What about writing to sophisticated audiences? Don't specialists prefer jargon when discussing their industry or trade?

Some argue that jargon is appropriate because it's language used by specialists in your target audience. But I think they confuse jargon with technical terms.

Technical terms are words or phrases that communicate a concept or idea more precisely and concisely than ordinary terms. Example: "operating system" to describe the software that controls the basic operations of a computer.

Jargon, on the other hand, is language more complex than the ideas it serves to communicate.

Example: I worked for a company that made industrial equipment. In one of our products, a door opened at the bottom of a silo, allowing powder to fall into a dump truck underneath. Our chief engineer insisted that in our copy we replace "dumped" with "gravimetrically conveyed."

For a client, I wrote that the dental brace they manufactured helped keep loose teeth in place. The product manager rewrote "keep loose teeth in place" to "stabilize mobile dentition." To me, this is like calling the sea shore an "ocean-land interface."

Mark Twain said "I never write metropolis when I get paid the same amount of money to write the word city." But is there an exception to the rule of writing the way people talk? A situation where you would deliberately use language more complex than the idea it serves to communicate?

Yes. The one case in which you might consider replacing ordinary language with more sophisticated phraseology is when you want to set your product *above* the ordinary.

Take a look at a Mont Blanc catalog. They don't describe their products as pens; they sell "writing instruments." Why? Because Mont Blanc pens start at about $100 ... and, while that's too much to pay for a pen, it's not too much to pay for a "writing instrument."

The goal of direct response copywriting is not to produce perfect prose or great writing. It is to persuade the consumer to buy your product. And the bottom line is: the copywriter should do whatever it takes to achieve that goal, whether or not writing purists approve.

For instance, grammarians dislike the phrase "free gift," complaining that "free" is inherent in the definition of gift: what gift isn't free? But in a recent lecture, my colleague Herschell Gordon Lewis defended "free gift" because it works, explaining that "each word reinforces the other."

I remember years ago hearing about a mailer who actually split test "free gift" vs. "gift." Not only did "free gift" win handily, but a number of recipients of the "gift" letter responded by inquiring whether the gift was indeed free.

Which reminds me of what Ralph Waldo Emerson once said: "It is not enough to write so you can be understood; you must write so clearly that you cannot be misunderstood."

78

THE 3 MOST IMPORTANT SKILLS FOR INTERNET MARKETING

When you hear about all the folks who are making thousands of dollars a week in passive income selling information products on the Internet … and "working" only a few hours a day …

… it's very tempting to want to chuck what you are doing and jump on the bandwagon.

But before you take the leap, it pays to think about whether Internet marketing is right for you.

On the surface, Internet information marketing sounds like everybody should be doing it.

Of course, if that happened, who would fix your car … or trim your hedges … or prepare your tax returns?

But not everybody is going to go into Internet marketing, of course — as tempting and attractive as it sounds.

Should you? Who else should? Who shouldn't?

To begin with, what you are selling as an Internet information marketer is useful knowledge on a specialized topic.

Therefore, if you already possess this specialized knowledge, you are in an advantageous position.

According to Gary North, most people in fact do have some specialized knowledge they can turn into a business.

"You possess a lot more knowledge than you think," says Gary. "In many cases, that knowledge is valuable to those who don't possess it."

If it's not immediately obvious to you what specialized knowledge you possess that other people would pay for, stop and take a personal inventory.

On a sheet of paper, list everything you know. Include your formal education ... degrees ... job history ... skills ... hobbies ... and interests.

One or more of the items on your list most likely can be the basis of a profitable Internet information marketing business.

Are you articulate? If you can express yourself well in writing or orally, that also positions you for success in the Internet information marketing business.

You do not have to be a brilliant orator or a great writer. You just need the ability to express yourself clearly and concisely in a pleasing manner that people enjoy reading.

The next thing that gives you an advantage in the Internet marketing business is a strong desire to make more money than you are now making.

Money is important, because there are a lot of people who write and publish stuff (blogs, articles, poems, books, fiction) with little or no concern about money.

These dilettantes (and I am using the word in its literal meaning, not as a pejorative) post their stuff on the Web and give it away for free.

Their reward is sharing and knowing that people are reading or looking at their work.

But putting up a Web site and posting content to it is easy. Getting people to pay you for it is a bit more of a challenge — and requires a lot more work than just giving it away online.

An interest in making money from your intellectual property will give you the impetus and motivation to do the extra work it takes to create and sell information products online — a process I teach in my Internet Marketing Retirement Program:

www.theinternetmarketingretirementplan.com

Have you studied copywriting? You do not need to be a good copywriter to have a successful Internet marketing business.

But you do need the ability to know whether a promotion written for you by a freelance copywriter is any good, so you can tell the writer how you want it fixed.

If you are a good copywriter, that's a bonus, because hiring top copywriters for landing pages and other sales copy is expensive — and by doing it yourself, you can avoid their fees.

Do you read marketing blogs and articles? If so, you have yet another advantage, because the key to success in Internet marketing is the marketing, not the content creation.

Quality content is important. But the people who make serious money online do so because they are good marketers, not because they are good writers or speakers.

Many people who love to write or speak are enamored with the "creative" part of communication, but aren't good at the business side of things. If you go into Internet marketing, you will have to pay more attention to the business side.

In particular, you need to know the numbers of Internet marketing and what you can realistically expect in terms of results from your promotions.

You do not need to have an aptitude for math, since the arithmetic of Internet marketing return on investment (ROI) is very simple and can be handled with a pocket calculator.

But you do need to be conscious of revenue coming in and money going out to cover expenses. Starting and running an Internet marketing business does not cost a lot of money, but the cost is not zero.

The one thing you absolutely do not need to start your own Internet marketing information business is knowledge of computers or technical ability of any kind.

The 3 most important skills for an Internet marketer to possess are (1) marketing, (2) copywriting, and (3) communication (the ability to create content in writing and orally).

I advise Internet marketers to outsource all technical tasks such as setting up their computer, installing their e-commerce software, broadcasting e-mail marketing messages, maintaining their subscriber list, graphic design of e-books, video editing, and designing landing pages and Web sites.

You can get people, both in the U.S. and especially overseas, to handle all these tasks at dirt-cheap prices. Go on Web sites such as www.elance.com and www.rentacoder.com and you can easily find all the help you need, at prices so low they will astonish you.

Even if you can do the technical stuff, I advise you not to. That's right. Throw away your copy of Front Page or Dream Weaver — and hire someone else to design that landing page. Why?

With the limited amount of hours available for work each day, you need to spend your time on tasks that give you maximum return on time invested (ROTI).

The tasks with the highest ROTI revolve around thinking about your business and planning new products and marketing campaigns.

The technical stuff has the lowest ROTI. To be frank, it's a waste of your valuable time.

And the less efficient you are in running your Internet business, the more difficult achieving the "Internet marketing lifestyle" — making a six-figure passive income working only a few hours a day — will be to achieve.

To summarize, ask yourself:

- Do I have useful knowledge of a specialized topic that people will pay for?
- Can I express myself clearly orally and in writing?
- Do I have a desire to earn more money from what I know?
- Can I develop some skill in copywriting?
- Do I understand the fundamentals of Internet marketing?

The more "yes" answers you gave, the better equipped you are to turn your knowledge into dollars.

79

BUILDING YOUR "SWIPE FILE"

A "swipe" file is a collection of promotions you have collected from other marketers.

"A good swipe file is better than a college education," says my old direct marketing professor, master copywriter Milt Pierce.

The swipe file provides inspiration and ideas from successful marketing campaigns you may be able to use in your promotion.

By doing so, it can help overcome writer's block. With ideas from a swipe file, you can write copy better and faster.

Lots of copywriters today keep swipe files of promotions in their industry, particularly health and financial writers.

Milt, however, preferred to get his inspiration and ideas from promotions for products different than the one he was writing about.

When a client who is selling insurance asked Milt to create a direct mail package, he would avoid looking in his insurance swipe file.

Instead, he looked in his swipe files for totally unrelated products. Why?

The reason is simple.

"If you create an insurance package that looks like every other insurance package, you're just being a copycat," said Milt.

"However, if you check through other types of packages, you're more likely to come up with an original approach to the insurance package."

A good example is a recent print ad I saw for the Stauer Titanium watch.

The ad shows a large photo of the watch.

The headline above it reads:

"We Apologize that It Loses 1 Second Every 20 Million Years."

The style and approach seem, to me anyway, to be inspired by the classic David Ogilvy Rolls Royce ad.

The headline for Ogilvy's ad for Rolls Royce was:

"At 60 miles an hour the loudest noise in this new Rolls-Royce comes from the electric clock."

If Stauer's ad was for a car, it would seem derivative of the Ogilvy ad — not very original.

But Stauer has created a compelling ad by adapting Ogilvy's straightforward, fact-based copy approach to a watch.

It's an approach not typically used in this category ... so it supports Milt's claim that applying ideas used in one industry to another can result in an interesting and effective promotion.

The best results I've seen from using swipe files have come not from creatively plagiarizing promotions within the same industry.

They've come from cross-pollination of ideas between different industries.

For instance, I was looking at my swipe file for options trading promotions to come up with ideas for a DM package to sell trading software.

Nothing. So I flipped through my other swipe files. In my health swipe file, I came across a promotion for a vision supplement. The headline: "Why bilberry and luetine don't work."

I knocked off the headline in my trading software promotion — and tripled the control.

My headline: "Why most trading software doesn't work ... and never will."

In a breakthrough fundraising direct mail package, the nonprofit sent a free paperback book to potential donors.

The slim "book" was actually a promotion written to solicit donations, and the package did gangbusters.

A major financial publisher copied the format — now known as a "bookalog" — to promote an investment newsletter.

The book they wrote and sent prospects, titled "The Plague of the Black Debt," was one of their most successful promotions of all time.

One interesting footnote to the Stauer watch swipe from the Rolls Royce ad....

David Ogilvy has been accused of stealing the headline for his most famous ad from another copywriter.

It was always believed that Ogilvy came up with this brilliant way of communicating Rolls Royce quality on his own — perhaps by driving his own Rolls.

I have also heard that he found the fact about the Rolls Royce clock in an article published in an automotive trade journal.

But now others are saying he took it from another car ad, for Pierce-Arrows.

And their headline, which was published years before Ogilvy's Rolls ad, indeed is remarkably similar:

"The only sound one can hear in the new Pierce-Arrows is the ticking of the electric clock."

I don't know whether Ogilvy had a swipe file and deliberately swiped the idea from Pierce-Arrows.

Today their ad is forgotten but his is one of the classic ads of all time.

Why?

I think the addition of "at 60 mph" makes the Rolls ad much stronger.

Back then, big cars were noisier than they are today, and a car that quiet at high-speed was a much more credible demonstration of quality than a car going 20 mph.

When you swipe from another industry instead of your own, you steer clear of copycatting and plagiarism charges — and are credited as brilliantly original when your swiped ad works.

80

CRAFTING YOUR ELEVATOR PITCH

An "elevator pitch" is a 30-second answer to the question, "What do you do?"

You need an elevator pitch because the question "What do you do?" is usually asked by complete strangers in casual circumstances.

In these situations, you do not have a captive audience watching you go through your PowerPoint sales presentation.

So your answer must be pithy and to the point.

Why does it matter how you answer the question "What do you do?" when speaking to someone you don't know?

Because you never know when the person you're speaking to is a potential customer or referral source.

Most elevator pitches, unfortunately, don't work — because they are straightforward descriptions of job functions and titles, generating not much else aside from disinterest and a few yawns.

For example, a fellow I met at a party told me, "I am a certified financial planner with more than 20 years experience working."

Yawn.

My friend sales trainer Paul Karasik has an antidote to the deadly dull elevator pitch.

Karasik's three-part formula can enable you to quickly construct the perfect elevator pitch.

By "perfect," I mean an elevator pitch that concisely communicates the value your product or service offers — in a manner that engages rather than bores the other person.

What is the formula?

The first part is to ask a question beginning with the words "Do you know?"

The question identifies the pain or need that your product or service addresses.

For a financial planner who, say, works mostly with middle-aged women who are separated, divorced, widowed, and possibly re-entering the workplace, this question might be:

"Do you know how when women get divorced or re-enter the workforce after many years of depending on a spouse, they are overwhelmed by all the financial decisions they have to make"?

The second part of the formula is a statement that begins with the words "What I do" or "What we do" — followed by a clear description of the service you deliver.

Continuing with our financial planner, she might say: "What we do is help women gain control of their finances and achieve their personal financial and investment goals."

The third part of the formula presents a big benefit and begins "so that."

Here's what the whole thing sounds like:

"Do you know how when women get divorced or re-enter the workforce after many years of depending on a spouse, they are overwhelmed by all the financial decisions they have to make?

"What we do is help women gain control of their finances and achieve their personal financial and investment goals, so that they can stay in the house they have lived in all their lives, have enough income to enjoy a comfortable lifestyle, and be free of money worries."

Action step: construct your elevator pitch today or tonight using Paul Karasik's three-part formula.

- First part: ask a question beginning with the words "Do you know?" that identifies the pain or need that your product or service addresses.
- Second part: describe your service, beginning with the words "What I do" or "What we do."
- Third part: explain why your service is valuable by describing the benefits it delivers, beginning with the words "So that."

81

THE AWFUL TRUTH ABOUT CONTENT MARKETING

Is content marketing — the marketing methodology that entails disseminating free special reports, white papers, e-books, blog posts, and other useful content to potential customers — overrated?

Sales expert Robert Minskoff seems to think so.

"Go ahead and blog, tweet, and post," says Minskoff. "But be very aware that there is still a large segment of the buying population that places very little importance on that type of content."

So what does work in getting the order? "Selling is a human interaction," Robert says. "Be human."

I am the first to stand up and say content marketing — which in the good old days, we simply called "free information offers" — can work well.

After all, I have been an active practitioner of content marketing since the early 1980s.

But content marketing has its limits.

Offering free content is great for generating inquiries — people love to get free stuff.

It also educates the consumer on how to buy your type of product.

For instance, say you offer a free report "7 Things to Look for When Hiring a Roofer."

Naturally, your roofing service precisely meets all 7 requirements spelled out in the report.

So after reading the report, homeowners will be more likely to hire you than your competitors who do not precisely match the requirements you listed.

However, if all you do is give away free content, you are not going to close many sales.

Content marketers need to remember that we are in the business of selling, not giving away free stuff.

The prospect is there not merely to be educated. You also have to sell him on why he should buy your product vs. other alternatives — including doing nothing. And that's not content marketing. That's copywriting.

To close the sale, at some point the prospect must receive a communication containing copy that (1) highlights your product's unique advantages over the competition, (2) overcomes his objections, and (3) proves that your product is a superior solution to his problems.

You may also need professional salespeople who know how to establish relationships with prospects, diagnose their needs, and convince them your company is the best equipped to meet those needs.

Not to be mean-spirited, but I think part of the reason so many marketers jumped on the content marketing bandwagon so readily is that writing content is a lot easier — and less threatening — than either writing copy that sells or selling in person.

It's a relatively easy and pleasant task to write a short blog post on a thought, idea, tip, or factoid that caught your fancy. Or put that information in your e-zine.

It's quite another to convince a terrific prospect to retain your firm when he is objecting that your price is too high — or he thinks your competitor is just as good as you are.

That kind of situation causes your average content marketer to run for the hills — but copywriters and salespeople alike relish such selling challenges. It's what we're paid for.

The bottom line: content marketing is fine as far as it goes. But nothing really happens until somebody sells something.

82

HOW TO GET OUT OF A SLUMP

I once gave a very well-attended course at the Learning Annex in New York City called "How to Get Out of a Slump."

I think the reason it was well-attended was because the topic is universal: everybody gets in a slump every now and then — not just baseball players.

To my great surprise, one of the attendees was a former star of a network sitcom.

She is beautiful and talented, but after the sitcom went off the air, her career (she told me) went into a long slump … and the success others had predicted for her did not materialize.

The entire essence of the course was a simple 3-step process:

1. Find out what works and doesn't work for you.
2. Stop doing what doesn't work.
3. Do MUCH more of what does work.

The importance of the word "much" in step 3 is critical.

When you have a setback, don't just try a few things to reverse it.

Take what I call "massive action."

Do much more than you think is required to reverse your slump.

That way, the odds of finding something that works are geometrically increased.

I have often said that the secret to having a pipeline full of leads for your business is to figure out how much marketing you need to get the number of leads you want — and then do double that.

Years ago, I interviewed Jane Trahey, a successful advertising executive in Chicago, for a career book I was writing.

She told me the secret to her success was having many balls in the air at once, which increased the chances that at least one would stick.

The natural tendency of human beings faced with difficulty and adversity is to shut down — to retreat and nurse their wounds.

The stereotype of this is the young woman who sits on the couch eating a large container of fudge ripple ice cream.

You must resist this temptation to give up and instead do the opposite — leap into action at full speed and full steam.

Be sure to follow my 3-step formula which requires you to (1) find out what does and does not work, (2) stop doing what doesn't work, and (3) do much more of what does work.

Remember the old maxim: Insanity is doing things in the same way and expecting different results.

It is also doing nothing.

By the way, worrying about the slump you are in is human nature, but it is also a complete waste of time.

So stop worrying about your slump. And start doing something about it.

83

ACTION VS. MOTIVATION

A lot of my subscribers ask me how I get motivated to do my work … but the truth is: I think the whole idea of motivation is overrated.

My subscriber RM writes: "Bob, thanks for balancing out the often severely unrealistic optimism that often comes with motivational literature … you're keeping it real."

A whole mini-industry, motivational speaking and publishing, has evolved to help people worldwide find their motivation.

But I believe you can do what you must do to succeed whether you feel motivated or not.

In an attempt at humorous marketing, an actor reading the script on a radio commercial pauses and asks his producer, "What's my motivation here?"

The producer answers deadpan: "We're paying you."

JH, a successful novelist, says that the secret to his success is that he writes every day whether he feels motivated to or not.

229

"Writing is my job," says JH. "If I work in the chicken plant, do I not go to the chicken plant today just because I don't feel like it?"

I also don't place overly much importance on positive thinking or optimism.

The book "The Secret" says that if you keep thinking positive thoughts, you will get or become what you think about.

Note: I well understand the Law of Attraction. Please do not write to me suggesting I do not and offering your explanation. I was listening to Earl Nightingale when many of my readers were in diapers.

The Law of Attraction notwithstanding, my experience is that ideas, visualization, affirmations, and positive thoughts alone are next to nothing. It is action that gets you the results.

I am by nature a pessimist. Dr. Martin Seligman, a psychologist and author of the book "Learned Optimism," says that an advantage of pessimists is that they see things realistically.

As a negative sort of person, I do at times wonder whether, in my large body of how-to writing, I may have failed to sufficiently motivate my readers. My writing tends to be long on actionable ideas and short on rah-rah talk.

Many info marketers motivate by promising outrageous results in their promotional copy and their products. A lot do so by hyping the business opportunity they are selling in their writings.

But unless the buyer follows the instructions given in the product and keeps at it, he is unlikely to achieve the results he wants.

I like what my colleague info marketer FG says: "I make no promises about your results. That's up to you."

Nike's iconic ad campaign encapsulates my advice to you: "Just do it."

Nike has it right. What matters most is not what you think or say; what matters most is what you do.

Thomas Carlyle said it this way: "Produce! Produce! Were it but the pitifullest infinitesimal fraction of a product, produce it in God's name! 'Tis the utmost thou hast in thee: out with it, then."

84

THE VIRTUE OF MODESTY

AL, a superstar stock broker on Wall Street, once said: "The more you tell the client that you are not a guru, not a rain-maker, the more credible you become."

I think this kind of humbleness goes a long way toward getting people to trust you. Yet modestly is a credibility builder that almost no one uses. What a shame!

For instance, on one of his Web sites, my buddy Fred Gleeck, the superstar information marketer, writes:

"Probably 98% of people who buy my products do nothing. The testimonials on this site represent those who HAVE done something.

"I make no promises about your results. That's up to you. The information is solid. The testimonials represent a VERY SMALL portion of the people who buy this product, much to my chagrin!"

This is brilliant because it is both honest and believable. The reader either knows or suspects that most information products don't deliver the results their authors boast about. Fred's copy resonates with the belief the reader already has in his head instead of clashing with it.

Fred also avoids creating unrealistic expectations on the part of the buyer. If you buy his product and don't get the results, you realize that it is at least in part your fault. So this reduces dissatisfaction and minimizes refund requests.

Sad to say, the majority of people I encounter both in business and my personal life are braggarts, to one degree or another.

To me, that's counterproductive, because in my observation, most people dislike braggarts and admire modesty.

The Bible, Jeremiah 9:23: "Thus saith the LORD, Let not the wise [man] glory in his wisdom, neither let the mighty [man] glory in his might, let not the rich [man] glory in his riches."

If you wish to be a humble and modest human being, or at least give the appearance of being one, here are 3 simple rules to follow:

1. Resist the constant temptation to brag, no matter how frequent or strong the impulse.

2. Do not tell people about your successes, accomplishments, or good fortune unless they ask. And even then, downplay it.

3. Is what you are about to say going to make the other person feel bad about themselves in comparison to you? Are you saying it unnecessarily to feed your own ego? If so, don't say it.

85

WHAT IT REALLY TAKES
TO BECOME A GURU

I once heard a professional speaker give this advice on how to become a guru in your field.

She said, "Read every book you can find on your topic, and in a year you will be one of the top experts in the field."

I think this advice is dead wrong.

Yes, someone who wants to become an expert should be a student of his discipline or craft: read the books, attend the Webinars, and take the classes.

But that's not enough: you must also acquire real-world experience by doing the thing you desire to become an expert in.

Study and reading provide valuable knowledge, but it is theoretical knowledge.

It does not become ingrained in your mind until you do what you are studying — multiple times.

To be a credible expert, you must do the thing you teach, not just read about it.

I advocate the 25-50-25 rule for becoming an expert in your topic:

- 25% of your time should be spent reading about and studying the thing you want to become an expert in.
- 50% of your time should be spent in practice — actually DOING the thing.
- 25% of your time should be spent observing others who are already successful at it.

A few years back, I took an adult education course on mail order so I could improve my mail order business.

The teacher was terrible and a student (not me) raised his hand and asked her, "Uh, Ms. H ... Do you actually HAVE a mail order business yourself?"

She turned beet red and admitted she did not. She had been "outed" and was embarrassed.

Knowing I was in mail order, she asked me to stand up and teach the rest of the evening, which I happily did.

I knew a writer, LW, who wanted to write a book on mail order, got a contract to do so, and then realized he had never done mail order, even though he had read a lot about it.

Admirably, he started a small mail order business to gain experience for writing the book.

Of course there are exceptions, but I personally like the credible gurus best.

In management, Peter Drucker was considered a guru, but he never ran a big company.

Jack Welch is also considered a management guru, but he was CEO of GE. Fortune Magazine named him "Manager of the Century."

Mark Ford says you need 1,000 hours of practice to get good at something and 10,000 hours to become a master. Malcolm Gladwell also says 10,000 hours.

Fred Gleeck has the 90/10 rule for determining whether you can call yourself an expert.

He says you don't have to be the best or most knowledgeable in your field.

All you have to do is know more about your subject than 90% of the people out there.

I have another formula that applies to gurus: the 1/3-1/3-1/3 rule. It says:

- 1/3 of the people out there are impressed by gurus and want to learn from them or do business with them.
- 1/3 of the people are indifferent to gurus: they don't care whether you're a top expert or not. They just want someone competent to get the job done.
- 1/3 of the people actively dislike gurus, thinking them phonies and blowhards.

A typical comment of resentment against gurus is: "That guy doesn't know any more than I do!"

The retort is an observation I read long ago: "An expert doesn't know more than anyone else; it's just that his information is better organized."

Even Jack Welch wasn't established as a management guru until he wrote a best-selling business book and lectured on management to thousands of people.

86

WHAT YOU HAVE TO BE
GOOD AT TO SUCCEED

Confession time: I am an inferior human being ... meaning I come up short in almost every category by which people are measured.

Every day, I look around and see people who are more athletic than me ... better-looking ... taller ... smarter ... thinner ... kinder ... more personable ... wealthier ... healthier ... more well-adjusted ... better parents ... better spouses ... even funnier.

Whatever I do professionally — copywriting, book writing, speaking, information marketing, consulting — there are others who are more successful and make much more money at it than I do (though in one of these vocations not many others and not that much more money).

How do I live with myself knowing that I am so inferior?

The secret is that you can be lousy at 99.9% of things and still have a happy and successful life — at long as you are good at just a few or perhaps even only one thing.

As far as I know, Paul Simon is good at only music. He's certainly not the biggest, strongest, or best-looking guy on the block.

Also, most fans listening to his music would agree that Paul Simon doesn't have the best voice and isn't the greatest singer in the world.

But Paul Simon has enough people who like his songs and his singing to give him a lucrative and successful music career.

You do not have to be the best there is at what you do to make a great living at it. SR is a great example.

SR is a professional stand-up comic who decided to make the transition to more lucrative performing as a corporate motivational speaker.

I have heard SR do both comedy and speaking. He is not the funniest comic I have ever heard. He is not the best motivational speaker I have ever heard.

But he IS the funniest motivational speaker I have ever heard. So he makes a great living speaking for meeting planners who want a motivational speaker who can also make their audience laugh.

What most people don't realize is that you don't have to possess nearly as many fans as Paul Simon to make a lot of money and live well from your work.

I think it was Seth Godin who observed that if you have just 10,000 fans, you can make a great living and have a successful career.

For instance, if you have an e-list with 10,000 subscribers, and can convince each to spend just $100 a year with you, you will gross annual sales of a million dollars.

Ten thousand people are hardly a big fan base; Bon Jovi probably has millions of fans. You do not need a huge fan base to succeed at whatever it is you do.

If you are a freelance copywriter, and tomorrow 10% of the Fortune 500 wanted you to write copy for them, you would be overwhelmed and could not handle a fraction of the workload — even if the other 90% of the Fortune 500 ignored you.

You simply do not need every company out there to consider you the top copywriter. You only need a few who like what you do well enough to want you to work on their promotions.

And even those few companies do not have to consider you the "best" at what you do. They simply have to feel that your service is a good fit for what they want.

Years ago, when I did some consulting work for Dow Chemical, they shared with me that they were producing 778 print ads, brochures, catalogs, press releases, data sheets, tech bulletins, case studies, and other marketing documents that year.

If you were a copywriter back then and Dow was your only client, they could keep you busy and profitable round the clock — and do the same for ten other copywriters at the same time. And that's just one client.

So if it helps you, I want you to know:

1. You can be middling to poor at most things and still have a successful life and career — as long as you are good at even just one thing.
2. You don't even have to be the best at what you ARE good at to have a successful life and career. You just have to offer something that other people want enough to pay for.
3. You don't have to have throngs of admirers. In many instances 10,000 fans, 100 customers, or 10 clients or less can keep you busy and profitable all year long.

If all this is of some comfort to you, and stops you from fretting about what you see as your shortcomings, then I have achieved my goal for this e-mail.

87

FIVE MISTAKE I WISH I HAD AVOIDED

I've made a large number of mistakes in my life. These flubs have cost me more in lost income, career success, and happiness than I could possibly keep track of.

Here are my 5 worst screw-ups, presented in the hopes that I can help you avoid making the same errors I did:

1. Not jumping on opportunities.

When Internet marketing arrived on the scene, I both resisted and ignored it.

I could have gotten into online information marketing in the 1990s.

Instead, I waited until 2004, until my colleague FG pushed me into doing it.

As a result, others gained the leadership position I could have owned, and I lost hundreds of thousands of dollars in sales I could have made during that time.

Joe Vitale and others have said, "Money loves speed." The faster you act, the more likely you are to succeed.

2. Not having an ultra-narrow niche.

At the beginning of my copywriting career, I wrote only industrial copy, and was well positioned in that niche. I loved it! Industrial clients wanted to hire ME, not my generalist competitors.

As time went on, more people outside that niche wanted to hire me, and so I became less focused, although today I do have four niches: financial, health, high tech, and business-to-business.

I love writing for the variety of clients I have today, but from a purely business point of view, life would be easier if I were more narrowly niched.

I think copywriters who laser focus on a narrow niche are smart, like Pam Foster who specializes in the marketing of pet products. Now that's a narrow niche!

3. Turning down book contracts.

There have been a few times over the last three decades when I turned down a major publisher who wanted me to write a book for them.

In each case I came to regret turning down the book offer — and wished I had accepted and had written the book.

Every book I have written has helped my career in some way — even my satire, sex, and Star Trek books!

My advice: writing traditional paper books is good for your career or business, so if you are offered a contract by a real publisher, take it.

4. Not saving your accomplishments and kudos.

Any time I get a letter of praise, I drop it in a file labeled "kudos." I then excerpt these favorable comments and post them on my site:

http://www.bly.com/newsite/Pages/testimonials.php

Any time you produce something for an employer or client, like a video or a brochure, save a copy as an electronic file.

Clients today increasingly want to see that you have done work similar to what they need done now.

The more samples you can show them, and the closer those samples match their current project requirements, the more comfortable they will be hiring you.

Although I saved a lot of my work, every once in a while a prospect asks for a sample in a field where I have done work — but don't have the sample. And I kick myself every time.

5. Not having children at an early age.

This we couldn't help: although I got married at 25, my wife was diagnosed with cancer a few months after the wedding, and we could not have kids for several years following her treatment. Then we went through infertility and didn't have our kids until we were in our 30s.

If I could change all that, I would have had kids when we were still in our 20s. Doing so increases the odds that the parents will be around for the kids and grandkids longer. And, younger parents have more energy.

Steve Martin became a first-time dad at age 67. When his daughter graduates college, her father will be 88. That's not ideal for either parent or child, in my opinion.

CONCLUSION

What is success? The precise definition is not important, because everyone does or should have his or her own definition of what success means for them. But it does mean that if you don't have a clear picture of what your life would be like for you to consider yourself successful, you need to create one. It's the old maxim: if you don't know your destination, how will you ever get there?

I once spoke before a group of hundreds of college seniors majoring in engineering. I asked them, "How many of you want to be successful?" Every hand in the room went up. I then asked, "How many of you can tell me what success is?" Only two hands went up.

You need a personal definition of what success would be for you. Mine is fairly simple: I want to do what I want to do, when I want to do it, where I want to do it, and with whom I want to do it.

Your definition of success might be to have a net worth of a million dollars, $10 million, or $100 million. That is not mine. My priorities are freedom and doing work I love. Yours may be different. Whatever they are, it's my hope that Bob Bly's Guide to Success makes it easier to get there.

4 BONUS REPORTS (A $116 VALUE)
— YOURS FREE

The essays in this book were originally published in my e-newsletter The Direct Response Letter.

You can get all my new essays for free without buying a thing by subscribing to my free e-newsletter now:

www.bly.com/reports

Subscribe now and you also get 4 free bonus reports totaling over 200 pages of actionable how-to marketing content:

- ** Free Special Report #1: Make $100,000 a Year Selling Information Online.
- ** Free Special Report #2: Secrets of Successful Business-to-Business Marketing.
- ** Free Special Report #3: How to Double Your Response Rates.
- ** Free Special Report #4: Online Marketing That Works.

Each report has a list price of $29; total value of this package of reports is $116.

But you can get all 4 reports FREE when you click on the link below now:

www.bly.com/reports

ABOUT THE AUTHOR

BOB BLY is a freelance copywriter with more than 3 decades of experience in business-to-business and direct marketing. McGraw-Hill calls Bob Bly "America's top copywriter." Clients include IBM, the Conference Board, PSE&G, AT&T, Ott-Lite Technology, Intuit, ExecuNet, Boardoom, Medical Economics, Grumman, RCA, ITT Fluid Technology, and Praxair.

Bob has given presentations to numerous organizations including: National Speakers Association, American Seminar Leaders Association, American Society for Training and Development, U.S. Army, American Society of Journalists and Authors, Society for Technical Communications, Discover Card, Learning Annex, and New York University School of Continuing Education.

He is the author of 80 books including *Selling Your Services* (Henry Holt; over 50,000 sold) and *The Elements of Business Writing* (Alyn & Bacon; over 100,000 copies sold). Bob's articles have appeared in *Cosmopolitan, Writer's Digest, Successful Meetings, Amtrak Express, Direct,* and many other publications.

Bob writes a monthly column for *Target Marketing* magazine. *The Direct Response Letter*, Bob's monthly e-newsletter, has 65,000 subscribers.

Awards include a Gold Echo from the Direct Marketing Association, an IMMY from the Information Industry Association, two Southstar Awards, an American Corporate Identity Award of Excellence, the Standard of Excellence award from the Web Marketing Association, and Copywriter of the Year from AWAI.

Bob is a member of the Specialized Information Publishers Association (SIPA) and the American Institute for Chemical Engineers (AIChE). He can be reached at:

Bob Bly
    31 Cheyenne Drive
    Montville, NJ 07045
    phone: 973-263-0562
    fax 973-263-0613
    E-mail: rwbly@bly.com
    Web: www.bly.com

Printed in the USA
CPSIA information can be obtained
at www.ICGtesting.com
JSHW022219140824
68134JS00018B/1148